education
begins
before birth

Omraam Mikhaël Aïvanhov

education
begins
before birth

New translation from the French
2nd edition

Collection Izvor
No. 203

EDITIONS PROSVETA

By the same author:

(translated from the French)

Izvor Collection

Prosveta S.A. – B.P. 12 – Fréjus, France

ISBN 2-85566-374-1

1ere édition : ISBN 2-85566-188-9

édition originale : ISBN 2-85566-208-7

TABLE OF CONTENTS

EDITOR'S NOTE

The reader is asked to bear in mind that the editors have retained the spoken style of the Master Omraam Mikhaël Aïvanhov in this presentation of the Teaching of the Universal White Brotherhood.

It should also be mentioned that the word 'white' in the name of the Brotherhood is not a discriminatory reference to the colour or race of its members. On the contrary: just as white light is the sum and synthesis of all the other colours, so the Universal White Brotherhood concerns all human beings of every race, nation or creed and invites them to unite in creating a new world of brotherhood and harmony.

1

THE FIRST PRIORITY : EDUCATING PARENTS

It is quite likely that some of you have wondered why, since I am supposed to be a pedagogue, I so rarely talk about how to bring up your children. This is the main concern of all other pedagogues, and I seem to be an exception. Why? The reason is simple: I believe that it is the parents who stand most in need of instruction.

I have no pet educational theory: I believe only in the educational value of the parents' behaviour, both before and after the birth of their children. This is why I have never said very much about how to educate your children. If parents do nothing to educate themselves, how can they expect to educate their children? People talk to parents about how to bring up their children as though they themselves already had all the preparation they needed. If people have children everybody takes it for granted that they are capable of bringing them up. But very often this is simply not the case: it is the parents, first and foremost, who need to be instructed and taught how to behave so as to be a beneficial influence on their children.

People who do not know my programme criticize me, 'A pedagogue? He's no pedagogue, he never talks about the education of children.' But they say this because they have not understood my point of view. As long as parents themselves are not up to the mark it makes no difference how many important educational theories you explain to them: it will do no good. Just the opposite in fact, because not only will they not understand, but if they attempt to apply your theories without understanding them they will do a lot of harm to their children.

How many people who decide to have children have ever stopped to ask themselves whether they are fitted to do so? Are they healthy? Do they have the means to provide for them properly? And, above all, do they have the qualities they need to be a constant example and to give their children security and consolation in all circumstances? They never even talk about it. They bring children into the world and leave them to bring themselves up. And the children do what they can on their own and then, one day, they too have children in the same deplorable conditions as their parents.

I am constantly astounded to see how many young men and women who want to get married have never paused to think about preparing themselves for their future role as parents. When one sees some young women who are pregnant, one cannot help thinking, 'But she's a baby herself, and look at her, she's expecting another baby!' It is written on her face: she is still a child. So what can you expect? It is far better not to have children if you are not properly prepared to do so, otherwise, I do assure you, it will cost you dearly.

You may ask, 'But what can I do to prepare myself?' The very best way is to make sure that your thoughts and feelings, indeed your whole attitude and way of life are such as to attract exceptional beings into your family. Yes: this is possible. Initiatic Science teaches that children are not born into a particular family by chance. Whether they realize it or not – and most of the time they are very far from realizing it – it is the parents who cause those particular entities to incarnate as their children. And this being so, they should consciously endeavour to attract divine beings, creatures of genius, into their family. They have this tremendous power, the power of choosing their own children – and most of them are totally unaware of it.

So the whole question needs to be re-examined from the beginning, and the beginning is the conception of a child. It never occurs to parents that they should prepare themselves for months and even years before performing this sacred act. Oh, no! As often as not, children are conceived after their parents have been out on a spree, eating and drinking too much. This is the occasion most parents choose – if one can speak of 'choosing' in these conditions! Why couldn't they wait for a moment of peace and lucidity, for a moment of deep and true harmony? But, no. They pick a moment when they are besotted by alcohol and not fully conscious of what they are doing. This is the sublime condition of many parents at the moment of conceiving a child! Have they never stopped to wonder what elements they introduce into a child conceived under these conditions? A child which comes into the world burdened with such elements is the first victim of its own parents. And now, who do you think most needs to be educated? I will tell you: the parents, not their children.

If parents quarrel, tell lies and cheat other people in the presence of their children, how can they possibly hope to educate them? It has already been ascertained that a baby can fall ill and show signs of nervous disorders when its parents quarrel. Even if it is not in the same room at the time, a quarrel creates a discordant atmosphere which the baby immediately picks up, for it is still very dependent on its parents. The baby is not consciously aware of the disharmony but this does not prevent it from being extremely receptive and its etheric body feels the shock.

Parents must be more conscious of their responsibilities. They have no right to invite spiritual entities to incarnate as their children if they are unfitted for their task. Sometimes I see parents behaving so unbelievably stupidly that I ask them, 'Tell me... do you love your child or not?' Of course, they get very indignant, 'What? Love him? Of course we love him!' But I am obliged to tell them, 'I don't believe it. If you loved him you'd change your attitude and start trying to correct some of the things which have such a disastrous effect on him. But you don't make the slightest effort. Is that your love?'

I know that the future of the Brotherhood lies with the children, but it is their parents that I am concerned with. I want to make them understand that they must not bring children into the world simply to satisfy an atavistic instinct of procreation. The instinct continues to exist, of course. But it is time that it was transposed onto a higher, more spiritual plane: the act of procreation should be accomplished with the full participation of your mind, soul and spirit and, in this way, your child will be linked to a world superior to our own. Most people are content to live like animals: they eat, drink and procreate like animals. There is no spiritual content to what they do. Love simply doesn't come into it. All they're interested in is pleasure, and for a few moments of pleasure they are going to have to pay – and their children are going to have to pay – for the rest of their lives!

Do you really want me to concern myself with your children? No. It is you who are my first concern and indirectly, through you, I am already doing something for the children you have now and for those you will have in the future.

2

EDUCATION BEGINS BEFORE BIRTH

Most people, when they decide to have a child, imagine that their powers are limited to performing the necessary physical acts, but that everything else: the child's physical constitution and character, his talents, qualities and defects, are a question of chance or of something they think of vaguely as 'the will of God'. They have heard about heredity, of course, so they fully expect their child to have some physical or psychological likeness to themselves or their own parents or at least to some member of the family. But they never imagine that it is within their power to increase or diminish this likeness or, more generally, to choose what kind of person their child will be. And this is where they are greatly mistaken: parents have a large part in determining what kind of person their future child will be.

But parents who want to give birth to a very highly developed being have to prepare themselves long before the child is conceived, because superior entities only consent to incarnate with parents who have already achieved a certain degree of purity and self-mastery. An entity of very high calibre will not choose a family for its wealth or renown, in fact it will be more likely to choose a family of modest means in which it will be less tempted to lead an easy life. What is important is to find a family capable of providing it with an heredity which will not be an obstacle to the accomplishment of the spiritual task for which it has decided to incarnate. Very few men and women can offer a very highly evolved spiritual being the conditions it needs to incarnate, and this explains why there are so few divinities in the world and so many very inferior people, so many criminals, so many sick people.

The Teaching of the Universal White Brotherhood, therefore, shows men and women in what frame of mind and in what state of purity they must prepare for the conception of a child. They can even choose the best moment for conception in relation to the most favourable planetary aspects. How did humans sink so low as to leave this all-important event, the conception of a child, to chance? It is something for which they should call on Heaven, asking the angels to come and help them to attract a powerful, luminous being into their family. But it never occurs to them: they look to alcohol for help and, very often, the man behaves like an animal, doing violence to his wife and arousing feelings of disgust and contempt and thoughts of revenge in her. In these conditions is it surprising if the resulting child is a monster?

Let's take a closer look at the subject of conception. For a child to be born into the world, the father has to give his seed to the mother who nurtures it and brings it to maturity. You could say that it is the father who creates and the mother who forms their child. The father's seed contains a condensation of his quintessence. All that he has experienced in the past as well as his present life is expressed in his seed. And this means, therefore, that a man can give a seed of greater or lesser quality according to the kind of life he has lived in the past and is living now.

I have often explained how everything we do in life is recorded within us, in the chromosomes of our cells. Every single cell has its memory and however skillfully you may play the part of decent, honest and charitable people when you are with others, it is what goes on inside you, what you think and feel in private, which is recorded and handed down from father to son, generation after generation. And if your chromosomes record disease or vice, once they have been handed on to your children, you can consult all the doctors and specialists, all the professors and schools you like, you will never find a cure for them. It is too late, the damage has been done. Everything is transmitted to your children and if it does not show up in the first one it will inevitably do so in the second or third child. You have to understand that Nature is always faithful and true to herself.

It would be a mistake, therefore, to think that what a man gives to his wife at the moment of conception is always of the same quality. If he has never made any effort to improve and purify himself he can only give his wife the seed of a very commonplace individual, perhaps even of a criminal.

Let's take an example: it is not a very poetic one, perhaps, but at least it has the merit of being perfectly clear. The function of a tap is to supply water, and that water may be crystal-clear or it may be clouded and muddy. A man who persistently harbours vicious thoughts and feelings can supply only dirty water, whereas one who works constantly for what is right and virtuous, one whose being is oriented towards the light will supply crystal-clear, life-giving water. So, do not be surprised: the quality of the seed which a man gives to his wife at the moment of conception depends on his degree of evolution.

Just as a seed planted in the soil is programmed to produce a specific tree or plant, the seed which a man plants in a woman is programmed to produce a child with specific talents and capacities or, on the other hand, with specific taints and weaknesses. During the nine months of gestation the mother supplies all the materials needed to carry out the programme: here too I can reveal some extremely interesting and important facts.

Throughout the nine months of pregnancy a woman not only forms the physical body of her child but, without realizing it, she influences the seed provided by the father by giving it conditions that will either help or hinder the development of its various qualities and characteristics. You may wonder how she does this. She too has to watch over her thoughts and feelings and the kind of life she leads. This is what I call spiritual gold-plating or galvanoplasty.

Let me begin by describing the electro-chemical process of galvanoplasty which is used in gold-plating and which, transposed onto the spiritual plane, can give results of tremendous importance for the whole of humanity.

Two electrodes are introduced into a solution of metallic salts: gold, silver or copper. The anode or positive pole is a sheet of the same metal as that in the solution, and the cathode, or

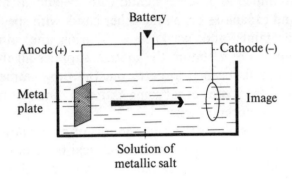

Solution of
metallic salt

negative pole, is a gutta-percha mould coated
with graphite and stamped with the design of a
medal or coin. The two electrodes are wired to
the two poles of a battery and when the power is
switched on the electric current causes a film of
metal to be deposited on the cathode and, at the
same time, decomposes the anode, thus providing a constant supply of precious metal into the
solution. Little by little, the cathode is completely covered with the metal and the results are
what you intended: a design coated in gold,
silver or copper.

If you observe what takes place in nature you will see that this process is not restricted to the man-made techniques of gold-plating: it exists on all levels. For instance, in the ocean of space, the planet earth represents the cathode or negative pole, the feminine principle, whereas the heavens – that is, the sun and other stars – represent the anode or positive pole, the masculine principle. There is a constant flow and interchange of currents and forces between the earth and the sun (and other stars) because they are both immersed in the cosmic solution: the ether or universal fluid which embraces and encompasses all the heavenly bodies. And the battery to which the two poles are connected and which sets everything in motion is, of course, God Himself.

And now, suppose we attach a mould of some kind, a seed for instance, to the earth: the seed, in close contact with the cathode (earth), is immersed in the cosmic solution and the current flowing through the solution from God produces the same results as in electro-plating. Particles of the materials present in the solution begin to build up on the seed, while the anode (the sun and the stars) constantly renews and regenerates the solution as the seed grows and draws sustenance from it. Every seed planted in the soil, therefore draws the elements it needs, according to its specific nature, from the surrounding ether and welds them to itself in order to grow and develop.

Exactly the same phenomenon can be seen in the process of gestation, for a pregnant woman also carries within her the seed, the electrodes and the solution. The seed, the living sperm implanted in her womb by the father represents the cathode and it bears a design or image which may be the portrait of a drunkard, a criminal or a perfectly ordinary and uninteresting being, or it may be the portrait of a saint or a genius. As soon as a woman is pregnant a current begins to flow between her brain (the anode) and the seed. The brain receives energy from the battery: God, the Fountainhead of cosmic energy, to which it is connected, and this energy flows from the brain to the embryo. The solution is the mother's blood in which both anode and cathode (the brain and the uterus) are immersed, for our blood bathes all our organs and cells and all the physical elements exist in solution in the blood including gold, silver, copper, etc.

The anode, therefore, supplies the precious metal (the mother's thoughts which decomposes in the solution (her bloodstream), thereby regenerating it. The seed implanted in her womb may be of very exceptional quality, but if she has 'leaden' thoughts in her head (symbolically speaking), she need not be surprised if, later on, her child is cast in lead, that is that he is vicious, pessimistic or sickly. You must realize that the seed is only the mould, and although it may bear the stamp of a magnificent likeness, if it is reproduced in base metal it will lose all its value.

But, suppose a woman knows how gold-plating is done and makes up her mind to apply the same rules in preparing to give birth to her baby : as soon as the seed (cathode) is implanted in her womb, she places a sheet of gold in her mind (anode), the gold of pure, lofty thoughts and feelings. The current is switched on and the blood flowing through her body conveys the precious metal to the seed. The child grows, clothed, as it were, in gold, and when it is born it is robust and healthy, beautiful both physically and in character and capable of overcoming all difficulties and diseases and all evil influences.

Most mothers have no inkling of the tremendous influence their inner state has on the child in their womb. Later, after it is born, they begin to take care of it and look for people to educate and instruct it and so on. But by then it is too late. Once a child is born the die has already been cast. No instructor or educator can transform a child who has received inferior elements from its mother while still in the womb.

A tutor or teacher can do a great deal for a child, but only in the way of instruction. They can never change his innate nature. If the fundamental nature of a child is defective it will never be anything else however excellent his educator may be. Whatever you do to lead, it will never be anything but lead. You can polish it, file it or slice a piece off it to make it shine : it will shine for a few minutes but, in no time at all, it will have become as dull and grey as before, simply because it is lead. You have to make your children of gold, not of lead, for even if a child of gold is obliged to live in the worst possible conditions he will never tarnish or be corrupted because the essence of his nature is pure.

Now you see why it is so vitally important for a pregnant woman to harbour only luminous thoughts. Thanks to her thoughts the seed that is growing within her will absorb the pure, precious materials she gives it and, one day, she will bring into the world a great artist or a brilliant scientist, a saint, a messenger from God. A mother can accomplish great miracles because she holds the key to the forces of life.

My mother told me that when she conceived me and, later, when she was carrying me, she did so with the idea of consecrating me to God's service. And, in fact, on the day of my christening the priest was so happy that he got drunk for the

first time in his life – normally he never drank!
Afterwards he said that he had drunk too much
because I was certainly not like all the other
children he baptized, and he prophesied something about me: but I am not obliged to tell you
what it was! Later I became a real rascal: I have
already told you how I used to steal apples from
the neighbour's orchard and light fires in barns!
But that phase did not last very long, because it
is the deeper characteristics which last: the
other manifestations are purely superficial and
transitory.

Not that I claim that, because my mother
consecrated me to God, I am somebody very extraordinary. You can consecrate your children
to God but you cannot know in advance what
level they have reached in the hierarchy of the
servants of God. Mothers can certainly not
know this and I do not believe that my own
mother knew. So the fact that she consecrated
me to God has no bearing on my own, personal
level. A great many Christians have been consecrated by their mothers and they spend a lot of
time in church but they never really improve
very much. The only thing one can say for certain is that their mothers asked that a tiny spark
should burn in them. If someone fans the spark
it becomes a blaze, but a spark amounts to nothing if it is not nourished. If you want it to grow

and spread you have to keep wood on the fire –
symbolically speaking.

It is well-known that many pregnant women
are subject to all kinds of whims and uncontrolled impulses they never normally have. But
what people do not know is why this happens. I
will tell you : a pregnant woman is often visited
by entities who look forward to having some
part in the life of her child later on, and they try
to influence the mother and interfere with the
gold-plating she is doing. They know that if this
is not done properly they will be able to go in
and out of that child and feed on him. When this
happens it is plainly visible in the child's behaviour quite early on in life.

Usually the children who come here take to
me at once but on three or four occasions there
has been a child who has tried to avoid me and
no one could understand why. But I knew why!
This kind of phenomenon holds no secrets for
me. The parents were very upset and unhappy
about it and I had to explain to the child's
mother, 'You see, while you were pregnant you
allowed yourself to do certain things which attracted these entities to your little one and now
they ask nothing better than to remain in him
and live off him. They are still waiting for the
right moment to come out into the open but

they know that I am their enemy. They know that once that child comes under my influence I will drive them out by my attitude, my will-power and by all that emanates from me. (In point of fact, I do nothing else: I spend my time driving out certain entities and putting others in their place. This is my greatest pleasure in life. You see, I have my pleasures too!) So this is why these entities try to keep your child away from me.' But I never accept defeat and, as I loved the parents, I decided to help them. I worked on the child and not long after, although he had always run away from me before, he rushed up to give me a hug. In fact you have sometimes seen this happening, haven't you?

During gestation, the mother must take great care to protect her child. Consciously, by her thoughts, she must create an atmosphere of purity and light around it so as to protect it from attack by harmful entities and, in this way, collaborate with the soul which is preparing to incarnate.

For, contrary to what some people believe, a soul does not enter a child's body during the period of gestation. It is perfectly true that, in its mother's womb, a child is alive: the heart beats and the embryo takes nourishment and grows, but the soul has not yet entered the body. It does this only when the child draws its first breath after birth. Until then the soul remains by the mother's side, collaborating with her in the work of building the child's different bodies (physical, astral and mental). Most women are not sufficiently sensitive or informed to realize that this work is going on within them. But even if they cannot see the soul of their child, they can at least talk to it and pray to it, saying, 'Here you are. I'll give you the best possible materials and I'll help you. But try to bring such and such a quality or talent with you so that my child will be an artist or a philosopher, a scientist or a saint.'

When a mother pronounces these words with all her heart they can be very powerful, truly magic, and she emanates certain particles that the spirit which is preparing to incarnate in her child can use as building materials in the construction of its different bodies. The child has nothing of its own, it receives everything from its mother. This is why she must be fully aware of what she is doing and make sure that she gives it only the most luminous and the purest possible materials.

All these phenomena which occur on the invisible level are unknown to most people. This is the importance of the Teaching: to make you sensitive to and aware of this subtle and intangible but very real world – the world that is more truly real than reality. Thanks to the Teaching, you are more aware of and more attentive to all the currents which influence you and all the entities which surround you. And it is this awareness which enables you to work for good.

Men and women must never forget that the children they will one day bring into the world will reflect their own mental attitudes, their own behaviour in one way or another. For whatever takes place in the heart and mind of a man always ends by taking physical shape. Every thought and every desire in a man's mind or heart is a living entity and your future sons and daughters already exist in advance, in your minds and hearts. So if your child is perfectly angelic as he grows up it is because he began as a splendid idea in your mind which has now become flesh and blood in your son and which will, through him, continue to help and sustain you. But if your child brings you nothing but trouble, you should understand that it is because he is the incarnation of a criminal idea which dwelt in you and was nourished by you in the past.

A child who comes into this world is not born out of nowhere. And if you ask me why your child was born I will tell you, 'so that you can see the living proof of what existed in your own mind.' This is how men and women get to know themselves : through their children.

3

A BLUEPRINT
FOR THE FUTURE OF MANKIND

Whenever any special problem arises on the national or international level various plans are drawn up to remedy it. Nowadays there are political, financial, economic and military plans of such vast scope and brilliant conception – it is quite amazing! One cannot help but marvel at them. The only trouble is that these wonderful schemes have never done much good because they only touch on the external, material side of things: technological improvements, increased production, the construction of more laboratories or universities, increased or decreased armaments, etc. And mankind continues to flounder along in the same old confusion and the same misfortunes. So seeing this I decided that I too would present my own plan, my own blueprint for the future of mankind. You will say: 'What conceit! What presumption!' You may be right of course but everyone has the right to draw up a plan, yourselves included, as long as it is useful and workable. And as you will see my plan is simplicity itself.

Instead of leaving the State to spend billions on hospitals, prisons, law-courts and schools, I advise it to concentrate all its attention on its pregnant mothers. The cost will be far less and the results infinitely superior. Therefore, I shall ask the State to prepare some building sites well oriented in relation to the sun and in some of the most beautiful parts of the country. And then, on these sites, I shall ask them to build houses in the styles and colours that I shall indicate. There will also be parks and gardens with trees and flowers, fountains and ornamental ponds. And all pregnant women would come and live in this setting for the whole period of gestation, with room and board paid for by the State.

In this way, their pregnancy would be spent in a beautiful and poetic atmosphere in which they could read, go for walks and listen to music. They would also listen to lectures which would teach them how they should be living this period of gestation : what to eat, but also and especially, the mental work they should be doing, the thoughts and feelings they should be using to influence and fashion their future babies. Their husbands would come and visit them, of course, and they would be shown how to behave with their wives so as to help them in their work. And you would see that in this way, given such conditions of peace, calm and beauty, women would bring children into the world who would be worthy channels for the graces and blessings that Heaven is waiting to pour out on humanity.

Whereas now, only very few of the spirits who incarnate in the present circumstances come from Heaven. Where do all the others come from? The doors are closed to heavenly spirits. It is not possible for them to incarnate in bodies which are prepared in impurity, vice and disorder. And this is why mankind is not getting any better. Of course it will get better, in the long run, but only after thousands of years during which it will have to experience great catastrophies and much suffering. All the changes that have taken place in recent years on the technical, economic or medical levels have not managed to improve the human race. It is still mired in the same passions and vices as before these so-called improvements. In fact it is even worse than before! And yet it is possible to improve mankind, but on one condition and that is that we begin at the beginning: with the expectant mothers.

If you only knew the conditions in which some expectant mothers live! They live in dark, confined slums; and it is they who have to take care of everything and put up with whatever comes their way. And, on top of it all, their husbands come home drunk or in a rage because they can't find work or because their workmates have insulted them, and so they take it out on their wives with abuse and even blows. You can imagine the frame of mind of women who are preparing to bring children into the world in such conditions!

Instead of building maternity hospitals for mothers it would be far better to give them ideal conditions in which to prepare to bring their children into the world. Once the babies are born they can go back to the slums if they have to: later on their children will build palaces for them! Why, yes! It is their children, with all the talents and gifts they have received, who will one day extricate their parents from their squalor.

No one pays any attention to the conditions in which women bring children into the world nowadays and when, as a result, crime, disease and insanity affect a huge proportion of the population, the State builds still more hospitals, prisons and reformatories and increases its police force, its doctors and its social workers. But none of this can do any good whatever. Even if billions were spent on so-called improvements in the field of psychological and educational care it still would not alter the quintessence that human beings have received from their mothers before birth. The only method which holds out any hope is the one I propose.

No educator, no doctor, will ever change the innate nature of a child. You can give him a little superficial varnish, but that is all. Any attempt to improve his character really boils down to a sort of taming or breaking in. Exactly the same phenomenon has been observed with primitive tribesmen : you can give them a veneer of education, teach them to eat politely and dress correctly, but it will not last. As soon as they get back into their tribal environment they revert to type. Similarly if someone is a born criminal or a born saint, no one will ever change him. Oh, superficially, perhaps, and for a brief while he can be influenced, but fundamentally he will always be the same.

A lot of people will probably object that my plan is not scientific, but they have no right to criticize before trying it out. Of course, it will not solve all the problems of the human race all at once. Several generations will be needed. Even if parents make a tremendous effort to purify themselves, they will never totally rid themselves of the heritage of weakness and corruption they themselves have received from their parents. But if they are watchful, in spite of a few bad elements which may manage to slip into their children, the positive aspects will predominate, even in the first generation. The second generation will be better and the third will be better still, and little by little all the defective elements carried over from the past will disappear. Some intelligent and responsible people are needed, therefore, who understand the importance of the work that goes on in a pregnant woman and how, when she knows the laws which govern the gold-plating process and is in a setting of care and affection and sustained by the appropriate material conditions, she can draw on a vast reserve of truly superior materials with which to form not only the physical body of her child but also its astral and mental bodies (emotions and intellect) as well.

Unfortunately I know in advance that my plan will be rejected. No one will ever take the trouble to take a closer look at it because the present generation has been so thoroughly trained and shaped by other philosophies that there is no room in their heads for this idea. Obviously I am not so blind as not to realize that if a mother has to leave home for several months it will involve certain inconveniences, but I do believe that just a little more love, intelligence and goodwill would soon find solutions to the problem.

What is essential in the immediate future is that these ideas should be accepted by orthodox science, and this is not the case, not by a long chalk! This was proved recently when one of our sisters went to hospital to have her baby. While talking to her doctor, she mentioned that she belonged to a spiritual Teaching in which she had learned that the mental activity of the expectant mother could greatly influence her baby. And do you know what the doctor's reaction was? He burst out laughing and said, 'Don't believe it! All that is utter rubbish. What can a mother's thoughts possibly do to her child?' So you see what the medical profession thinks of this. And to think that a lot of people expect them to light the way for humanity!

It is true that some biologists have experimented with mice and found that fear and anxiety experienced by a pregnant female had repercussions on its offspring. But they insist on talking only about mice! They study mice rather than women, although women have been bringing children into the world for millions of years. Before we know it, the mice will be teaching human beings what is true and what is false. Scientists have built laboratories in which to study their mice and are tremendously proud of them, whereas they totally ignore the great laboratories of nature, which have always existed and which are far better equipped than ours. It is the evidence provided by mice that counts. I tell you :

it is mice who will point the way for humanity!
And what about women? Isn't it most insulting
for them? They should protest indignantly!

As far as I am concerned I prefer to leave
mice alone. I have observed a certain number of
pregnant women at various moments and then,
several years later, I have observed their children and I have seen that the problems and wor-
ries experienced by the mother at a particular
stage of her pregnancy are reflected in the life of
her child in the corresponding stages of its development. But we are still waiting for the official,
scientific verdict from the mice and, in the
meantime, the world has been peopled by monsters. Even if biologists have at last understood
that what is true for a mother mouse is even
truer for a pregnant woman – and it is by no
means certain that they have understood – they
are still far behind because their methods are so
slow that if they undertook to re-educate mankind it would take centuries! But don't delude
yourself into thinking that they will lift a finger
to enable women to benefit from their findings!
All they are interested in is their mice. They are
not interested in advising women about what to
do during pregnancy.

And this is why I launch this appeal to wom-
en throughout the world, 'Stir yourselves. Wake
up to the task that God has entrusted to you.

You have untold secrets in your keeping which could be used to regenerate the human race. But you are still unaware of these things. The time has come for you to be conscious of your mission and ask your menfolk to prepare the best possible conditions for you so that you can accomplish your great, magical work.' Of course when they hear that many women will say, 'We have shown our love and tenderness for hundreds of years but men have never understood us. They have only scoffed.' Yes, I know. Most men behave like selfish children, but if they are like that it is because women have never known how to play their part as mothers: they have not applied the technique of gold-plating while they were carrying their children, and now they have to put up with the consequences.

Nature has given women special powers but they used them badly or not at all. It is important that they become aware of these powers and realize that the future of the human race is in their hands. If women take the trouble to understand what I am saying they will become an unheard of force in the world, capable of sweeping all before it. But to achieve an exalted ideal they must be united. At the moment they are dispersed and disunited except in their readiness to seduce men! This is why they are not very powerful yet. From now on, all the women of the world must unite for the regeneration of the human race. In spite of all their intelligence and skill men cannot do very much in this way. It is women, mothers, who have been entrusted with this mission, for it is they who have been given the power of influencing the child in the womb.

This is why I appeal to you, all the sisters of the Brotherhood, to become more aware of the immense task to which you are called, and to awaken this consciousness in all the women in the world who still know nothing about it. This ideal, the desire to be useful will fill your hearts and souls and spirits. Inspiration will never desert you. Your hearts will know joy and you will feel rich because the ideal of contributing to the happiness of mankind will sustain and nourish you. Nothing will ever really satisfy you until this ideal is firmly anchored in your soul. However wealthy you may be materially you will always feel empty and discontented. The only thing capable of making you happy, radiant and full of light is to do what Heaven expects of you and fulfil your God-given mission.

4

DON'T NEGLECT YOUR CHILDREN

A certain number of changes have taken place in human society recently, and they are not all conducive to the education of children. More and more women, for example, are employed outside the home. They want the same independence as men and, as a job provides them with this independence, they all want a profession. But their profession obliges them to neglect their children who come home from school and find no one at home: father and mother are both at work. So the children get along as best they can; and they get along very well indeed when it comes to getting up to mischief in the absence of their parents, who become more and more like strangers to them.

I am not saying that mothers should not work. All I am saying is that these new social patterns are having certain effects on the education of children. As an educator I am obliged to recognize these effects. I am not giving advice to

anyone. Everyone has to sort out his own problem for himself, but I believe that, for children,
nothing can substitute for the presence of their
mother in the home, on condition, of course,
that she be really and truly present and capable
of playing her part as educator of her children.

You will say, 'Yes, but this change of mentality is also due to industrialization and technical
progress.' Of course. It is always the same: people always put the blame on external factors. But
technical progress need not necessarily have led
to the catastrophic situation in which human beings find themselves today. It is men and women
themselves, by reason of their ignorance and
egoism and their unbridled appetites, who have
got themselves into this situation. Everybody
blames the conditions, but who creates the conditions? They did not just drop from Heaven!
Technical progress is a good thing. It could have
lightened men's burden. Why did they have to
spoil things so that now it absorbs all their energies and has brought them to the edge of disaster?

In any case, nothing can justify parents in
leaving their children to their own resources or,
on the pretext that they are too busy, in leaving
them in the care of others: a servant, a neighbour or anyone else. Why did they bring their
children into the world? If they do not want to

look after them they would have done better to
leave them where they were. Parents who behave like this are going to be taught a hard lesson and it will come to them through their own
children. It is they who will bring suffering on
their parents for it is the parents who have called
them into this world and provided them with
their bodies, and the least they can do is to look
after them and not shift the burden on to someone else. The Lord alone knows what nonsense –
or even what filth – other people can put into
the heads of your children! I do not need to spell
it out for you.

Parents are so harebrained! Instead of
breast-feeding her baby herself, a mother will
hand it over to any wet-nurse with an abundant
supply of milk, without a thought for the disease
or vices that woman could communicate to the
baby along with her milk. A baby absorbs something of the character of the woman who nurses
it. This is why it is so important for mothers to
nurse their own babies because, while they are
nursing them, they can also, consciously, give
them a lot of love. If they do this their children
will never abandon them or make them suffer
because in absorbing their mothers' milk they
will also absorb their love.

And now, just reflect for a moment on this:
before her baby is born a mother nourishes it

with her blood, but once it is born she nourishes it with her milk. Blood, which is red, symbolizes life, strength and activity, whereas milk, which is white, symbolizes peace and purity. Milk represents a principle of harmony which complements and counterbalances the purely biological tendencies represented by blood. And this is why children who have not been breast-fed by their own mothers are not capable of manifesting themselves ideally, later on. The milk of another woman, or animal's milk, does not contain the same elements as that of the mother.

Through her milk, a mother gives her baby the love and tenderness which are vital to its proper development. This is why she must take care not to give it the breast when she is angry or in a negative frame of mind. The negative vibrations will poison her milk and her baby will receive elements which can make it physically or psychically ill. Nursing mothers should be very vigilant and prepare themselves in advance so as to be in the best possible frame of mind when they feed their children.

A great many mothers, for reasons of 'aesthetics' or other, purely frivolous reasons, give their babies a bottle – or get someone else to do so. And they, in the meantime, are free to go dancing or to a cocktail or dinner party. That is much more fun, and then, too, their breasts are reserved for the pleasure of a grown man, their husband or lover! It seems that breast-feeding spoils their beauty. There are so many deviations and disorders in this area nowadays! And this is why more and more children are becoming estranged from their parents: because they have never been nourished either with love or with their mothers' milk. Believe me, I am not inventing all this. These are facts which have already been verified.

When a woman nurses her baby she must do so with conscious attention, thinking of him and talking to him and, in this way, she gives him something of her heart and soul, of her own quintessence. A child who is nourished in this way will love his mother for all eternity. Even if she is ignorant and not very beautiful he will adore her. A child must be conceived in love and nourished with love. But I am afraid that the consciousness of most mothers is still too narrow and personal. They have not yet understood the importance of their mission as educators. No one pays any attention to true education and this is why everything is going from bad to worse.

Look at what happens to children who have been deprived of their mothers' and fathers' love and left to other people to bring up. In the United States you can see them hanging about on the streets, waiting for some man to come and pay to sleep with them. Hundreds of children, eight, ten and twelve years old have become street walkers. Before, it was mostly the girls, but now even very young boys are doing it too. And if you ask them why they accept to go with those men, they will tell you, 'Because they're kind. It's not so much for the money, but they give us a little affection and our parents beat us and threw us out of the house or abandoned us.' Of course children need to be loved! And suppose we began to see the same thing happening here, in France? The day will come, you may be sure. For whatever happens in America ends by happening, sooner or later, in France too.

Look after your children! Don't neglect them. I know that a lot of parents, nowadays, think that education is useless. They are convinced that a child should be left to develop on its own without outside interference which would run the risk of destroying his originality: his qualities will appear quite naturally if he is left entirely free. This is a very grave mistake! Heaven and Hell both lie dormant in every child and his future depends on whether his parents stimulate and develop the one or the other. I mentioned, one day, the example of a young girl, pure, innocent and beautifully brought up: she looks 'as though butter wouldn't melt in her mouth', as the saying goes. But if she gets worked up and finds herself in a situation where her sexuality is aroused, you will be dumb-founded to see what that angelic creature is capable of! All human beings are capable of every evil and of every good. It all depends on the conditions in which we find ourselves and the tendencies which have been cultivated in us.

Human nature has two faces, two sides to it: one is celestial, divine and the other is hellish, diabolical, and depending on the method parents use in educating their children, they encourage one aspect or the other. If they are not very careful they will see to their sorrow that they have brought out the evil aspects of their children's characters. Great vigilance and care are needed, especially while a child is still in the formative years. While he is growing and not yet fully formed he is full of energies which are looking for a direction and this is no time to be blindly trustful and to think that you have brought a little angel into the world. He will become an angel, certainly, as long as you are vigilant, intelligent and wise. But if you are careless and ignorant you will see: he will become a devil!

5

A NEW UNDERSTANDING
OF A MOTHER'S LOVE

I

I would like to tell you about the case of a young girl for whom the spiritual life was all that is most important and precious. She used to spend a lot of time in prayer and meditation and she was in the habit of practising various spiritual exercises in order to come closer and closer to the high ideal she had chosen. And then one day she married and had a baby, and from then on she has given priority to her married life: her husband and especially her child absorb her attention and she has abandoned all the rest. And now I would like to analyse this attitude for you.

Of course, I know that everybody will approve of this young woman's behaviour. It is only normal that she sacrifice her spiritual life in order to take care of her baby: after all, she is its mother. Every father and mother will be on her side : nothing should take priority in a mother's

heart over her own child. She should even be
ready to break the laws of God for the sake of
her child. And if her baby falls ill or dies it
would be normal for her to be very angry with
God and accuse Him of cruelty and injustice.
All of this corresponds to what people think a
mother's love should be and everyone agrees
that it is admirable. Everyone except me, that
is! I don't think it is admirable at all, for if a
woman is so attached to her child as to neglect
even the Lord, all it means is that she is thinking
of herself, not of her child.

Oh, yes! This is as clear as daylight to me! If
she neglects the realities of Heaven in order to
devote herself to her child what she is actually
doing is depriving him of the divine life, which is
the only true life, and making it impossible for
him to benefit from this immense reservoir of
light and peace. In the stupidity of her love she
snatches her baby away from his only sure haven, the only place where he could find happiness and immortality. She may believe that she
is 'looking after' him, keeping him safe from all
harm: in reality she is putting him in danger of
Hell itself, since she is cutting him off from all
beauty and harmony. Can you see this? Can you
see that there is a basic misconception here
which has prevailed in human society for thousands of years? A mother who loves her child

must never turn him away from Heaven, for Heaven is man's only haven, the only place in which every one of God's creatures is destined to find fulfilment. If she neglects God and thinks only of her child, her mind will no longer possess all those subtle, imponderable elements which flow from the realms of Light, from the Godhead, and consequently whatever she gives her child will be lifeless.

A mother who abandons the habit of constant reference to God is incapable of radiating the living, glowing particles which her child needs if he is to become a truly worthwhile human being. If she starves and impoverishes herself, obviously she will have nothing to give her child. Her love for him becomes something completely commonplace, and her child will be commonplace too. He may be healthy and well-dressed but if he is cut off from God he will never become more than a mediocre human being. Whereas a mother who really understands the teaching of Initiatic Science will constantly refer to God in her thoughts and prayers, 'Lord, I turn to Thee for light, love, health and all the beauty of Heaven for my baby.' And when she turns back to her family, she will be in a position to communicate to her baby a wealth of subtle, nourishing elements which other mothers have never heard of nor imagined because they have

no time to pray or meditate. They do have the
time, but their egotistical love excludes them
from adhering to this philosophy. This is why
the world is peopled with mediocre men and
women.

A mother should never do anything for her
baby without first turning to God to receive that
which she can then communicate to her child.
Why does she imagine that if she turns her attention away for a few minutes he might die? No!
Even if her baby were in danger of death while
her attention was concentrated on the Lord,
when she gets back to him she will rescue him.
But if she neglects God because she is afraid to
leave her baby alone, the day he is really in danger she will be incapable of doing anything for
him.

As long as parents are so attached to their
children that they cannot bear to leave them
while they go and improve their minds, they will
never be capable of transforming them nor of
making them really happy. It is impossible to
transform one's family if one is always with
them. It is not a question of leaving them physically, but of leaving them mentally. In other
words it is a question of abandoning one's mistaken notions of how to love and understand
them. 'But this is a crusade against our children!' you will say. Not at all. In fact it is quite

possible that I love your children more than you do. It might be worth analysing that! If anyone loves your children it is I : you do not really love them.

I knew a boy once who demanded money from his mother to pay for his extravagant tastes and threatened to kill himself if she refused. His mother simply said, 'Go ahead, my son. The world doesn't need people like you. I hoped you'd be a great and noble human being, but you behave like an utter scoundrel. Go and commit suicide. That's the best thing to do. I'll thank God when you're gone!' Well, thanks to his mother's courage, the boy began to take stock of himself and became a truly remarkable man. Years later he would say, 'It was my mother who saved me!' But if she had panicked and given way saying, 'Oh, my poor boy. Don't do that. Here's your money,' she would have turned him into a confirmed criminal.

And this is exactly what most parents do, their love is so blind and they are so weak-minded and flabby that they turn their children into criminals. 'But we love them!' They try to justify their lack of firmness and psychology in bringing up their children with that excuse, 'We love them!' instead of saying, 'How weak and foolish we've been,' they say, 'We love them.' I am the only one who does not believe them.

Half-hidden by the cry, 'We love them,' I can hear a little voice which murmurs, 'How stupid we were!' That is what I hear.

Abraham loved Isaac but he was ready to sacrifice him to show God that he loved Him even more than his own son. The question as to whether one loves God more than one's own son is always topical, but it never occurs to mothers and fathers to ask themselves what their own answer would be. God wanted to put Abraham to the test and He asked him to sacrifice his only child. You say, 'But why did He do that? Didn't He know perfectly well what Abraham would do? Why did He have to test him? Of course the Lord could read Abraham's mind and heart and He knew in advance what he would do; it was Abraham who did not know which love was strongest in him and he needed to know this. That is why God tried him. The test was not for the Lord's benefit but for Abraham's.

As a matter of fact all the trials God sends us teach us about ourselves. It is we who have no idea how much we can endure and how intelligent, strong, generous and kind, or how weak and stupid we are. We delude ourselves. We say, 'I've overcome this weakness, that vice, I love God above all things,' and then at the first little trial that comes along, we throw in the sponge! And we never understand why. Abraham found out that he loved God above all else, God had given him his son and he knew therefore that God could take him away.

Why do mothers not follow the same reasoning? They think they are acting for the good of their child in abandoning the Lord. They think that the protection they give him will be enough to keep dangers away. But what protection can they possibly give him if they themselves are not protected? They have turned theirs backs on the one, universal Protector. What pride and conceit!

Abraham was an Initiate, he did not rebel against the Lord, he prepared to sacrifice his son but God is not a blood-thirsty monster and at the last minute He provided a ram to replace Isaac on the altar, because Abraham had found out exactly how far he was prepared to go in sacrifice and that was all that was needed. If a mother is not ready to go to the same lengths and accept the same sacrifice, it shows not only that she is not very intelligent but also that she is too proud. How can she dare to imagine that she knows better than God Himself whether her child should live or die? With such a limited conception of love she will never be able to help her child, because instead of leading it towards the Light she will lead it away. In her mind it is her mother-love which takes priority. It is everything to her. In thinking this she is making a big mistake and, one way or another, she will have to pay for it because she will fail to do her duty. Her duty was to stay symbolically speaking, in Heaven, and to lead her child to Heaven with her.

You must never abandon Heaven for the sake of anyone, not even for your child or your husband or wife, because it is only if you are firmly rooted in Heaven that you will be able to do them any good. If you abandon the Light to please another human being, you will lose both Heaven and earth and those for whom you have given up so much will never belong to you, you will find yourself alone. You must seek Heaven, then you will also possess the earth, for the earth is always in attendance on Heaven as its faithful subject and servant.

If you allow sentimentality and blind attachment to predominate, not only will you not help others, but you yourself will suffer. To avoid this you must give first place to intelligence and wisdom; God Himself must be foremost in your heart, and when this is so whatever you love will be yours – even other people's children! Yes, for the children you love with a divine love belong to you far more truly than to their own mother if she loves them foolishly. You may say, 'But that's impossible! They are united by the ties of blood relationship...' True, but I assure you that blood relationships do not necessarily form the strongest ties. There are others that are more important.

The only beings who will ever belong to you are those you have learned to love, whether they be children, men or women. Outwardly, family ties are strongest but it often happens that different members of the same family have practically nothing in common because they belong to different spiritual families. You can belong physically to a family of peasants for instance, and spiritually to a royal family. Or the reverse: you can be physically a member of a royal family while in reality you belong to a family of miserable tramps!

If his family is in dire need, how will a father who truly loves them react? He will have the courage to leave them for a time and go and earn money in a foreign country. Whereas another, who is not motivated by the same kind of love, will not have the courage to leave his family. The former appears to be abandoning his wife and children but in fact he only leaves them for a time in order to help them: he goes abroad to earn a lot of money and when he gets back they can all be happy together. Whereas he who doesn't have the courage to leave condemns

both his family and himself to permanent pover-
ty. And now let me interpret this for you : a true
father and a true mother will 'abandon' their
children at intervals and, by means of prayer
and meditation, travel to 'distant lands' to amass
a fortune, and when they go home again their
whole family will be better off. Parents who
don't understand this will perhaps be constantly
with their children, but what can they give
them? Nothing but a few odds and ends, a few
mouldy crusts of bread!

True fathers and mothers often 'go abroad'.
For how long? It depends, for half an hour or an
hour, sometimes for a day or even a few months.
And when they come home again they share
their wealth with their children. You must admit
that I have arguments that can stand up to all
your 'logical' objections. And if any of you who
are mothers don't agree with me, you can come
and talk to me about it! I shall tell you, 'You
claim to love your child, but just analyse your
love. If you really love him you'll go 'abroad' for
at least ten minutes or half an hour every day. If
you do that then no matter what happens your
child will always have an abundance of what he
needs.'

II

A mother may do everything for her child, tirelessly loving and caring for him night and day, and yet, in spite of all her devotion he may never turn out to be anything special. In fact, he may grow up to be a good-for-nothing or even a criminal. How can this be? The reason is that she has never learned to project her love out beyond this world, to the higher spheres where she could find other, subtler elements to give to her child, elements that would actively influence him as he is growing up and help him to become someone really exceptional. How can any mother be so foolish as to suppose that, in spite of her ignorance and the narrowness of her mental horizons, in spite of being interested only in the most prosaic and commonplace pursuits, she can provide a child with the elements it needs in order to develop into someone capable of working wonders for mankind and the whole of human society?

As long as mothers make no effort to reach out to the highest levels and draw down particles of light, purity and eternity, whatever else they may do, their child will receive only the most common, ordinary elements from them. It is not quantity that is important, but quality. And it is this, this superior quality, which they must reach out for and communicate to their children. Look at it, if you like, in terms of mathematics: no amount of two-dimensional figures can produce a three-dimensional figure and no amount of three-dimensional bodies can ever build a four-dimensional body. In other words, no amount of ordinary, commonplace human beings will ever produce one genius and no amount of geniuses will ever produce one divinity. To produce a divinity you have to add other elements from another dimension, elements which can only be found in the spiritual, divine dimension. It is essential to understand this.

Mothers must learn, therefore, how to form and fashion their children. From time to time, several times a day, even if only for a few minutes, they should raise their thoughts to the Lord in prayer and ask Him for what they need: 'Dear Lord, You know that I want this child You have given me to be Your faithful servant. Please! Give me the sublime elements which only You can provide so that I can pass them on to him. Without them he will come to no good and that wouldn't be to his advantage, nor to mine nor to Yours!' And the Lord will scratch His head in perplexity and then send some of His faithful servants to help that Mother.

Does my way of explaining things startle you? Well, that doesn't matter. What does matter is that you understand and make progress, even if my explanations are very unorthodox and unacademic and not at all literary or philosophical! For my part, I want to do everything possible for mothers: I have tremendous admiration for their capacity for sacrifice. But they must open their minds to much wider horizons and learn to work for their children with new, spiritual methods. They still think that it is in their power to give their children the care and sacrifice they need, but this is not so: it is not enough. In truth it can never be enough: other forces and energies, other divine particles will always be necessary. A child who is nourished and impregnated by these divine elements every single day, will grow up to be a cause of wonder for all men.

You will say that it is not so easy to go and find God; but this is a figure of speech! Simply by thinking about the heavenly dimension a mother draws subtle elements to herself and passes them on to her child. Cases in which a mother's love was strong enough to snatch a child from the jaws of death have already been seen. The mother's love was so intense that it transformed something in her child : it generated currents so powerful that they were capable of expelling the negative, harmful elements that had invaded his body and saved his life. Obviously, cases like this are exceptional, but even if they can't always expect such dramatic results, mothers have a great many opportunities in everyday life for demonstrating their love for their children.

In the mornings, when we all go up to the *Rocher** to see the sunrise, for instance, I am always very moved to see so many mothers with their babies and I would like to tell them how to make their work more fruitful. Instead of walking about with your babies, to keep them quiet or put them to sleep, sit down quietly somewhere and talk to them, 'My little darling, my love, my treasure, my own beautiful baby...' When you murmur words like this to your child you are doing what the sun does : bathing him in light and warming him with your love. Simply

---

* The *Rocher* is the large rock at the top of a hill close to the Bonfin, where the Master and his disciples gather to see the sunrise.

by the power of your love you are calling all the angels and archangels to come to his aid. Then, too, you can speak to God, 'Lord, let this child be Your servant. Let him be the most beautiful, the most radiant and luminous, the most intelligent and the healthiest...' and in saying these words you picture your baby bathed in all that splendour.

The imaginative powers of a woman are very strong and she can use them to fashion her child and as all her hopes and prayers, all her feelings for him, are recorded by his etheric, astral and mental bodies, when she does this she not only gives great impetus to his evolution but she also creates a very strong bond between her child and herself.

One of the main reasons why relations between parents and children break down so frequently these days is that parents have become incapable of influencing their children by their own vibrations. They have become incapable of impregnating them with their love, wisdom, strength and life. How is it that mothers have not understood this a long time ago? Oh, it is true that, from time to time, if her child is ill or when he cuddles up to her and kisses her, a mother feels a little love for him, but that kind of love is without power, for other feelings take its place almost at once. It is so terribly rare to find someone who knows how to work on their children with intelligence and in full consciousness.

Well, there you are: this is how mothers should envisage their work when they go up to the *Rocher* at sunrise. If they do so this way they will be astonished to see that their love makes them tireless, for it is love that stimulates and nourishes the cells of the brain.

In a lecture about the power of thought and of the word, I explained how to influence your child by talking to him while he is asleep. Even if he neither hears nor understands, there are certain laws of the universe which will cause the seeds you plant in him to germinate and bear fruit when he grows up. You can talk to him about the moral laws and all that is good and true and you can be sure that everything you say will be recorded within him. Besides, who can be absolutely certain that he does not understand what you say? He cannot express himself yet, or show that he has understood, because his organs are not yet fully formed but this does not necessarily mean that he has not understood.

The spirit of even a mentally handicapped child is just as powerful and intelligent as any other, but it cannot manifest itself because the brain or the physical body is damaged. Take the greatest virtuoso in the world: if you give him a piano which is out of tune, will he be able to play? Of course not. But this does not mean that he is not perfectly capable. All it means is that the piano is in very poor shape. Well, our piano is our brain. This is the instrument by means of which the spirit manifests itself, and even if its owner is a genius and a virtuoso, if his piano is out of tune he will never be able to make beautiful music with it. Perhaps it is like this with children. They see and understand a great many things but they cannot express themselves. One hears of some amazing, totally inexplicable cases. There are a great many mysteries still about babies which have to be cleared up in the future. We still know so little about them! Sometimes, just for a few moments, one sees a fleeting expression of such intelligence on a baby's face that it leaves one speechless. And then, the very next second, the usual baby-expression is there again. I love to watch children: for me, they are like books and I can read so many things in them.

And now, let me say just one more word to mothers: do you really want your child to be a servant of God, a genius, a saint, a splendid human being, a benefactor of mankind? If so, look after him with all the love of which you are capable. Love is all-powerful. Talk to him while he is asleep, caress him gently, permeate him with Light of every colour: red, orange, golden-yellow, green, blue, indigo and purple. But be careful with the colours. If you want to become familiar with the true colours contained in the light of the sun you must use a prism, for the only way to see the full beauty and strength of nature's colours is with a crystal. In this way you can contemplate them for a long time and, later, reproduce them in your imagination. Be sure not to work with other, impure colours but only with those of the spectrum : they are the only true colours.

So try to permeate your child with these dazzling rays of coloured light. Imagine that the vibrations penetrate all the cells of his body. When you do this you are reproducing the greatest mystery of creation, that by which the Lord Himself penetrates and vivifies all of matter.

6

THE MAGIC WORD

It is truly amazing how many deviations one finds in the attitudes of parents towards their children. On the pretext that a child is too young to realize what goes on around him, they feel free to do and say all kinds of things and to behave abominably in his presence, without ever imagining that it can have a very harmful effect on his psychic health. For a child is extremely vulnerable, extremely impressionable, and it often turns out that certain maladjustments which only show up later in life have been caused by conversations or events that went on around him while he was still a baby.

Also, a great many parents do not pay enough attention to the way they talk to their children. They keep telling them they are incapable and stupid, and in the end the children are conditioned into being really incapable and stupid. Parents who do this are unaware that words are powerful, active forces and that what they say to their children can have tremendous influence on them. Why are they always threatening them with monsters? Why do they have to tell them that a policeman will arrest them if they're naughty and disobedient? Why are they always heaping reproaches on them or even cursing them for the slightest thing they do wrong? Don't they realize that the result will be that their children will go through life feeling threatened and insecure and end up as neurotics?

Parents must learn to use the power of words so as to do only good to their children, and I can give you a method for this. It is a method which is particularly for mothers with small babies. While her baby is asleep a mother should go and sit by its cot or pick it up and hold it in her arms, and talk to it very softly, 'My baby, I love you very much. I want you to be full of radiant light, divine life, intelligence and strength, purity and loving-kindness...' She should talk to her baby in this way of all that her heart desires for him. It is more than likely that some people will think this is nonsense, but I know that those who are conversant with the laws of the universe will agree with me, for they know that the Word is all-powerful. Even if the baby understands nothing, his mother's words will be recorded in his subconscious and will influence and guide him towards the marvellous future she has dreamed of for him.

A mother should do this every day and every evening. She should talk softly to him, gently stroking his head, telling him of the strength and all the virtues and qualities which are already his and which he will learn to develop later on. She should talk to him about his future, about how happy he is going to be and how he will become a noble, exceptional being. She should murmur only poetic, wonderful words to him.

Generally speaking, parents wait for their children to reach a certain level of intellectual understanding before they begin their education because then they can explain things to them, and they think that that is what education is all about: explanations! But this is not so: explanations have never had much educational value. The only valid educational method is example, showing children in very concrete ways what they should do by doing it in front of them, without explaining anything at all. Show them how to wash and clean, how to tidy up, how to prepare a meal. Children are little monkeys: as soon as they see you doing something they will copy you.

And if some of you say, 'Well, before doing as you advise, I'd like to understand exactly

what takes place and what processes are triggered on the etheric plane', all I can say is that if
you never act until you've seen and understood
every possible repercussion beforehand, you will
have to wait centuries! And in the meantime
your child will have grown up to be a good-for-
nothing. Don't wait! Take care of him right
away, for you have a very great responsibility.

What is so wonderful, too, is that when you
say those magic words for your baby, all kinds of
colours start to glow and radiate from you, from
your heart and your head, and certain entities of
the invisible world may be attracted by all this
beauty and decide to stay with your child and
work on him. So, I beg you, keep your intellect
quiet for a change and believe what I am telling
you, instead of forever voicing objections and
questions; it will be to your advantage and,
above all, to the advantage of your children. Do
any of you know all the laws of the psychic and
spiritual world well enough to be in a position to
doubt what I am telling you? As long as you are
still ignorant you need to believe and follow
someone who has gone further than you on the
path of knowledge. So, I repeat, 'Mothers, talk
to your babies even if they're asleep, even if they
can't understand.' Some of you may be in the
habit of talking to your children mentally, without words. But this is not enough. There is a

tremendous difference between a thought and a word.

One day I was giving a lecture in Amsterdam and there were several representatives of different spiritual and esoteric movements in the audience. Amongst other things I explained that meditation engenders enormous accumulations of psychic energy, and that many people who only meditate and never give expression to their meditation in words, end by being disturbed by those energies, simply because they have given them no other outlet. When you meditate, therefore, you should always formulate a few words so that the entities and forces mobilized by your meditation all converge in the direction indicated by your words. But, you may wonder, why are words necessary? Is thought alone not tremendously powerful? It is. But if you restrict yourself to thoughts without words it is like writing all kinds of promises and commitments on paper and then not putting your signature to them. Your promises are valid only when you sign. You can declare or promise whatever you like, and bequeath your fortune as you please, but if there is no signature on your will no one will take any notice of it. In the eyes of the world it is the signature that counts, and in spiritual work words are a signature.

When I explained this, the President of the

Anthroposophical Society of Holland exclaimed, 'Oh, but this is something new to me!' And he was very pleased to learn it. You see, there are a great many people who do not know this. Words are very important. You can think for hours on end if you like, but if you want to trigger something, to set something in motion so that your thought takes shape here on the physical level, then you need the intervention of words. Thought is powerful on the psychic level, but words are powerful on the physical level. And now, assimilate this truth and make it your own and you will see that you will get excellent results. Just a word of warning, though: do not formulate any words until a vital, living thought has taken shape in your mind and is supported by a strong feeling, otherwise your words will be hollow and ineffectual, and will produce nothing.

Even the children who are listening to me here today can assimilate a little of what I am saying, it is being recorded in their subconscious and although they cannot understand it today, later it will come up to the conscious level and they will be in a position to benefit from it. They will be far better able to use it and to succeed in life than those who have been excluded on the pretext that they were too young.

And the same is true for the children who

come with their parents to be there when the sun gets up : some people think they would be better off in their beds. Not at all ! Even if they go to sleep on the *Rocher* they will still absorb the ambiance of prayer, meditation and contemplation all round them and receive the benefit of the sun's rays. Never forget, the sun's rays are conscious, spiritual entities which caress and influence the children, and leave their mark in their etheric bodies.

A few years from now, when their playmates try to persuade them to get up to mischief with them, these children will feel something holding them back, an inner strength that will keep them on the path of purity, light and wisdom. Even if they have no idea where this deep-seated strength comes from, they will continue to feel its active influence. And in this way a child's education begins long before his understanding has developed.

In fact, I will go much further than that : I have already told you that once a child is born it is too late to begin his education. Yes, already then a child's parents no longer have the power to influence him decisively. They must begin before birth, even before he is conceived ! True education, the only kind of education which is really potent, efficient, real and indestructible, begins before a child is conceived.

My pedagogical ideas are new, I know, and often bizarre. But they get results. When you give a child something to eat he has no notion of the different kinds of energy his food gives him nor how this energy will contribute to his physical, moral and intellectual development. But nobody in their senses would wait for a child to understand before giving him something to eat! In the same way you should not wait before giving him divine, spiritual food. If we waited for children to be capable of understanding the spiritual life before giving it to them, they would soon be dead – spiritually dead. And this is what often happens : people wait for their children to be old enough to receive a spiritual education and in the meantime let them get so deeply accustomed to a mediocre way of life that when they want to correct the situation it is already too late. Nothing can be done.

7

NEVER LET YOUR CHILDREN BE IDLE

I am sure you must have noticed today how proud the children were to sing for us. It was a very serious matter for them. Oh, yes! They have done something really important today and they will remember it all their lives: they have sung in front of an audience! Possibly for you it was not noteworthy, but if you were capable of looking into the hearts of those children you would see that for them it was a great event. And now it is up to you to encourage them, tell them that it was a magnificent performance and that they should learn more songs because we need to hear them sing again.

It is very important to awaken the desire in children to become as good as possible in some activity. It is the best way of preventing them from getting up to mischief and wasting their time aimlessly. A child should never be allowed to be idle. Very often, when you want a child to keep still, you say, 'Be good'. But what has

goodness got to do with keeping still? It is not
surprising if, later on, they cannot bear 'goodness'. In their minds it is associated with immo-
bility and boredom and children are dynamic!
In fact, instead of telling them to keep quiet it is
far better to give them something to keep them
busy.

Parents should realize that it is normal for a
child to have to work hard to get his homework
or other little jobs done. A child has such immense reserves and such stamina that he soon
forgets any pain involved. But with every effort
he makes he is forging his character and this
should make his father and mother happy. Instead of which, very often, they say, 'Poor little
fellow, he mustn't tire himself', and this attitude
simply helps him to become weak, lazy, in-
competent and egotistical. That is parental love
and pedagogy for you! The children who climb
up to the *Rocher* to see the sun rise every morning: are they to be pitied? Are they unhappy because they are not in bed? Absolutely not. They
are happy, look at them! Parents should realize
that it is often they themselves who keep their
children weak and dependent. They should
change their attitude, otherwise they will suffer
the consequences for the rest of their lives because their children will grow up to be capri-
cious and egotistical adults.

I know many parents who made this mistake with their children and are suffering because of it, and all I can say is, 'It's your own fault. You should have started teaching your children to help you to wash a few plates and lay the table, or do some other little job very early on'. Obviously, most jobs in the house are too difficult for toddlers, they have neither the strength nor the ability, but they can watch you : you can do something in front of them and tell them, 'When you're bigger you'll do this or that.' And, in the meantime, there are all kinds of little things they can do to help, only the trouble is that parents do not give them anything to do because it is so much quicker and easier to do it oneself than to show a child what to do and then keep an eye on him while he is doing it ! But this is not a good educational method for later on when you want him to do something he has not learned to do when he was very small, he will not want to. His faculties were not trained early enough. And, when this happens it is no good scolding, 'Lazy bones ! Go and do this or that, try to learn', he will not want to. It is too late.

There are a certain number of good habits you should teach your children while they are still very young because then they will never lose them. I once met a man who had been to prison several times for theft and he admitted that even in prison, he always said his morning and evening prayer. It was a habit his father had instilled into him when he was still small and he could never forget it. So I asked him, 'You mean that you pray every morning and evening and yet you go on stealing?' 'Ah, yes', he replied, 'but that's different.' For him praying and stealing were not incompatible. Of course, it would have been better if his father had given him the habit of not stealing!

People do not realize how terribly strong a habit can be. If a child is used to his parents giving in to his slightest whim it is inevitable that later on, even when he is in the wrong and knows it, he will go on expecting everyone to let him have his way. By then it will be too late to change him. A child who has been pampered and spoiled will grow up always demanding the same treatment. Unfortunately, once he has grown up there will be only one force capable of educating him and that is life itself, for life is quite ruthless. So then he will suffer and learn better. But what a lot of unnecessary suffering parents store up for their children simply by giving in to all their wishes!

This is why I often tell parents, 'Take care, take care! Your kindness is really weakness and ignorance in disguise. Later on it is you who will be reduced to tears because you will be the first

victims of your own misguided kindness.' So
many parents come and complain to me about
their children's attitude! I am obliged to tell
them that they have brought it on themselves
and, of course, they do not understand. You
must never be weak with children because if you
are they will abuse your kindness and it will not
be their fault but yours. If no one shows a child
that there are certain rules which he must learn
to obey, and if while he is still very young he has
the impression that everything can be made to
give way to his every whim, how can you expect
him to listen to someone who tries to remon-
strate with him? He will refuse to obey and it is
normal. He wants to defy everyone, to destroy
everything, to destroy himself even rather than
give way. This is what he has been accustomed
to, it has become a habit and it is not his fault.

So, when parents realize that the mistakes
they have made in bringing up their child have
damaged his character, they have only one re-
course and that is to call on Heaven and the
spirits of wisdom to teach him a lesson which
will make him think. Their child will cry a little
and they will console him, but he will have understood, and in this way, after a few good lessons, he will be saved. I have often watched parents with their children and I have seen that it is
kindness, misguided kindness, that encourages

vice. Kindness is wonderful, but only so long as
it is subject to wisdom.

One day I was with a wealthy and distin-
guished family. They were very worried about
their only son who was giving them a lot of trouble. They spoiled him and gave him a lot of
money and he obviously neglected his studies
and spent all his time amusing himself. I wanted
to be of some help, so I said, 'Do you want to
save your son? If so, first of all, you must realize
that he has no gift for studies. If I were you I'd
apprentice him to a garage with a very strict boss
who would make him work, and I'd stop giving
him all that money. The easy life is bringing out
the worst in him.' I explained all this to them at
great length but they did not understand me. In
fact they were insulted by my advice because
they felt that it would be humiliating for them if
their son became a mechanic. They were count-
ing on a brilliant career for him! So, they did
not listen to me. They continued to send their
boy to the best schools in France and abroad and
to pay for the very best tutors for him and, above
all, they continued to spoil him with money and
expensive presents.

A few years later, the situation was so bad
that they remembered my advice. But I had the
surprise of my life when I heard what they had
done: instead of sending their boy as an appren-

tice in a garage as I had advised, they bought him the biggest, most modern and most expensive garage they could find! Obviously nothing in his previous experience had prepared him to run a business like that and before long the inevitable happened, he went bankrupt and his parents lost enormous sums of money. There is no point in telling you all that happened later. The point is that here is an example of parents who brought suffering and misfortune on their son through their weakness and foolish love.

Nowadays, parents no longer have the courage to use educational methods which forge a child's character. They say, 'They musn't be made to suffer. They must be given everything they want.' Well, it is this weakness which spoils their children and the day will come when they will be unable to get them to do anything they ask. In fact they will find themselves faced with gangsters who will ride roughshod over them and give them some very hard lessons, all because of their mistaken notions about education.

But parents refuse to trust me. They think I am being cruel. I am not being cruel : it is simply that I know a few rules. And these few little rules turn out to be major laws! In the past people brought up their children according to these laws, even kings, for kings always had wise old men in their palaces to advise them. One of

these sages might for instance have given the
king some advice about how to bring up his
child, 'Your Majesty, you have a son who is destined to reign after you. Will he be a just, honest
and impartial ruler? This is what you should
do : before he is old enough to realize that he's a
prince and heir to the throne, send him to live in
a poor family so as to learn how men and wom-
en suffer and struggle to survive and how hard
they have to work to earn a crust of bread. When
he comes back and ascends the throne he will
rule his people with justice, clemency and mer-
cy.' Some kings actually followed this advice.

But nowadays wealthy families do not want
to send their sons to learn a trade in hard or
painful conditions, they prefer to send them to
the capitals of the world or to Switzerland to the
most expensive and reputable boarding schools
where they hobnob with princes, playing tennis
and skiing and swimming. And when they get
back home they are wrapped in cotton-wool.
That is how these very 'intelligent' people bring
up their children.

Whereas it would be far better if someone
who is very rich did not let his children realize
it, otherwise they will never make an effort to
learn how to get on and make their own way in
life. A child who is used to wealth thinks that all
his wishes should be granted, that he has the

right to taste all the pleasures of life, and he grows up to be indolent and slothful. This is the worst possible kind of upbringing. So, as far as possible, parents should keep their children in ignorance of the wealth they will have when they grow up. Once they have acquired good habits of work and self-control, their parents can talk to them about the money they will inherit later, but not before.

If you think about it, this is what God Himself does with His children. He is the greatest educator, the supreme pedagogue, He never reveals the heritage that He has prepared for us on high. He lets us believe that we are poor and miserable so that we shall work and make a real effort on our own, and when, in toil and tears we have become worthy of our heritage, He reveals all the treasures He has in store for us. At that point we understand the wisdom of the Father who reveals none of this to us in advance. Initiates, who endeavour to work in the same way, also conceal many things from their disciples so that they will develop and grow strong.

Parents who want their children to assume important responsibilities in the future must bring them up to experience the difficulties of life, for otherwise how will they understand the difficulties of their subordinates, their workers or soldiers, in later life? Those who start life in very poor environments and pull themselves up by their own hard work, understand and are compassionate towards others who suffer, because they know what it is to suffer. Whereas those who are raised in cotton-wool are like Marie-Antoinette who said, 'They have no bread? Let them eat cake!' She simply did not understand.

8

PREPARE YOUR CHILDREN
FOR ADULT LIFE

I know that the philosophical questions which interest the adults here are not very entertaining for children and adolescents. They are much more interested in other activities or amusements. But still, the very fact of being here amongst adults who endeavour to put the Teaching into practice in their lives, means that it is all being recorded in their subconscious minds, even if they cannot yet understand the full, deepest significance. Later, when they have a serious problem to resolve, they will be in a better position than most to choose the right line of conduct, for they will have received an orientation and a stimulus towards what is right. It makes no difference that, at the moment, they are unaware that anything is going on. All that they have seen and heard will continue to influence them for the rest of their lives. And this is why the young must take part in our work.

Even if you have the impression that your children are too young, you should begin to prepare them now for the life they will lead later on, and they will gain a deeper understanding if they are in the company of adults and see how they live. Children themselves feel this need to prepare for adulthood: look at how a little girl instinctively wants a doll to cuddle and wash and feed. She is preparing herself for her future role as mother. Something within her spurs her on to explore the terrain in view of the future. This is a topic which is worth investigating.

Some children go to church with their parents without understanding much of what is going on, but the solemnity of the service and the recollected attitude of the adults make an impression on their souls which they will be able to understand more fully later on in life. Others may be taken to the funeral of a member of the family or of one of their little friends and they begin to wonder what happens to people who disappear. Death is an event they will inevitably come up against at some stage and it is useful for them to be prepared at an early age. The same is true for so many of the events of life. Every child is, to a certain extent, obliged to face up to events which are still in the future and, in this, he must be helped by the experience of adults.

Take another perfectly simple example: a chemistry student begins by learning what has already been discovered in his field up to the present. Later on, if he is capable of doing so, he will add his own discoveries to the existing sum of knowledge but, to begin with, he must study the experiments and discoveries of other chemists before him. If he decides to ignore them he might take twenty or thirty years to discover that a molecule of water is composed of one atom of oxygen and two atoms of hydrogen; and he may never even get that far. It is wiser to save time and accept the findings of one's forerunners.

If a child is accustomed to living with adults he will already be prepared to face certain events when they come along. He will remember what he saw his parents do and will do the same. This is why it is very good for young people not to be restricted to activities conceived for their age-group. One day I was talking to a woman who had two lovely daughters of about fifteen and I said, 'It would do your girls good to come to the Brotherhood and hear the truths which will be of use to them later on in life.' And do you know what her reaction was? 'Oh, no. They're too young. At their age they should be having fun. They love dances and surprise parties. They'll have plenty of time in the future to think about serious things!' Well, there you have a mother who is preparing a disastrous future for her children.

Of course young people must be allowed to dance. I am not against dancing! But they must also get into the habit of thinking about a higher order of things. Human beings are not made only for work, effort or serious reflection, that is clear enough. In fact, in the past, it was the Initiates who established the days of popular rejoicing so that, with their dancing and singing and masquerading, people could give vent to the energies repressed by constant work and the cares of everyday life. On the other hand, if someone thinks that what is essential is to have fun and amuse oneself all the time, then he has completely missed the point of life!

I have no quarrel with a mother who wants her daughter to have a good time. I want to have a good time too. I never think of anything else! But there is more than one kind of 'good time' and you must be aware of the danger of any good times that are not offset and balanced by reflection. It will not be long before that young girl whose mother told her to go out and have fun, is soiled and 'devoured' by the first blackguard to come along and, as a result, not only will she lose all her freshness and charm but she will also lose her lucidity. In no time at all she will have gone to swell the ranks of those women who go through life with no notion of what it is all about.

Don't jump to the conclusion that I am narrow-minded. No one is more broad-minded than I am. I would like all young people, boys and girls, to be gay and to dance and sing. But at the same time, I would like them to study the science of the Initiates and to learn to forge bonds with the exalted, vivifying forces of nature. If they do this they will become marvellous men and women, capable of acting for the good of their family and country and even for the whole world.

So, there you are: just a few words to explain that one must not let young people do only what pleases them or is agreeable to them at their present stage of development. They must always be helped to aim a little higher, a little further, and to anticipate the future. Oh, I know. A lot of children anticipate, but not always in the best way. A darling, graceful little girl, for instance, has one ambition in life: to be like her aunt with lips and nails painted bright red and rings on all her fingers. Or a little boy dreams of being like his grandfather because he smokes a pipe and has an enormous walrus mustache! Without knowing it, young people often anticipate. They are in too much of a hurry to grow older and look important or blasé. If they only knew! They need not hurry: it will happen soon enough without any help from them! If there is anything that is absolutely certain it is this: nothing can prevent them from growing old!

In fact, young people should try to stay young as long as they can. In their hearts, I mean: spontaneous, uncomplicated and smiling. Personally I prefer to stay a child. I do everything in my power to maintain the spirit of childhood in me. The young want to grow old and I want to stay young. Youth vanishes so soon. It is like the Spring – all too brief!

9

PROTECT YOUR CHILDREN'S
SENSE OF WONDER

Look at these children listening to me: if you only knew how well they understand what I am saying! Their little faces vibrate. When it is time to laugh, they laugh and when it is time to think, they think. They react magnificently. As an audience they are much more satisfactory than adults! God alone knows what is going on in their little heads, how they see and understand things. Perhaps they get at the truth at once, whereas it takes you ages to get there. In fact I am sure they do perceive truth more quickly and more accurately than adults.

Children say a lot of things which adults find absurd because they don't understand and I have often been astounded by the depth of perception revealed by a child's reflection. They are natural and uncomplicated and still in touch with the heavenly regions they have come from. But their families and society in general inculcate their own logic, their own distorted view of things into their children who end by accepting them. Parents often deform their children's minds.

Very young children have an innate sense of the marvellous. They believe that everything is alive and intelligent. They talk to insects, stones, animals and plants. If they fall and hurt themselves on a stone they give it a kick or scold it because they think it hurt them deliberately. And if you tell them fairy tales full of giants and fairies and extraordinary beasts, it is wonderful to see how they believe it all. But only a few years later they will have lost their sense of wonder because adults laugh at their credulity or if they do not actually laugh at them, their materialistic attitude rubs off on the children.

Once a child has lost his sense of wonder he has lost his most precious faculty. For you cannot think that it is any great proof of superiority for adults to maintain that the universe has no soul and no intelligence, and that man is the only living creature who has the power of thought. The whole of nature is alive and intelligent and peopled with living, intelligent creatures many of whom are far more intelligent than man! As soon as a man rejects and denies that the whole of creation is alive and intelligent, death begins to get a hold on him. If you believe that everything around you is endowed with intelligence and life, then both intelligence and life will grow and increase within you.

Psychologists and educators should take a good look at this notion for they have not yet really studied the magical power of an idea. If you think that everyone on earth is evil, depraved, ugly and criminal-minded you are putting yourself in great danger for not only will it reflect on you but sooner or later you will actually end by being like that yourself. And if you believe, on the contrary, that you are surrounded by light, beauty, splendour and nobleness, this will influence you and little by little as the days go by, you will become more and more beautiful, expressive and noble of character.

Never kill a child's sense of the marvellous. In fact you should cultivate it so that it nourishes him all his life long; legends and fairy tales are good because they keep the sense of the invisible world and all its inhabitants alive in a child's mind.

When I was a child there were a few very old people in the family whose words expressed great wisdom. They were not educated people, most of them had never been to school (in a tiny village in rural Macedonia more than a century ago that was not unusual), but their whole attitude expressed such dignity and self-control that I admired them enormously. They were models for me. When they came to see us at home (I was six or seven years old) I was always delighted to see them and listened to them with rapt attention. I always asked them to tell me a story, and one of them in particular – called Mikhaël – made a deep impression on me. He was very wise. When he talked he would measure his words and gestures. Like my grandmother, he would tell me fantastic tales of battles between the forces of good and evil, the powers of light and darkness, white magicians and sorcerers! Good always triumphed over evil in the end. Ever since, I have felt that by means of these tales this old man and my grandmother gave me an impetus towards good and the light, and sowed in my heart a yearning to see the triumph of light over darkness.

I can see now that all this was planned: I had to hear those tales for they left a deep impression on me. Everything I learned later in books or at the university has been forgotten, the thing I remember is these tales in which the powers of light always triumphed over darkness.

Parents and relations influence children a great deal. For this reason you should be careful never to leave your children with anyone who might tell them all kinds of bad things. When they are small, everything they see and hear leaves an imprint on them which will last all their lives. So, watch over your children and in fact, if you can, you should choose their play-mates and always know who they are with. Look back at your own childhood years and you will probably find the reasons for your present tastes and tendencies, your present behaviour.

Childhood determines the whole of one's life. The impression received in childhood can never be erased and this is why adults have such an immense responsibility. If they damage a child with their vulgarity and ugliness he will bear the mark of it for the rest of his life. Adults must keep a strict watch over their behaviour for fear of giving a child an impetus in the wrong direction.

But you must understand me correctly: you also have to know certain laws of initiatic psychology. I am not saying that children should be raised in a dreamlike, poetic, imaginary and un-real atmosphere. Not at all. That too would be very dangerous. Every method has its good and its bad side and you must know how and when to apply it. Parents and educators must stimu-late a child's intellect and his practical intelli-gence, they must teach him to manage for him-self on the physical level and prepare him to cope with the realities he will meet later on in life, but they must never kill his taste for the marvellous or his sensitivity to unseen realities.

They should talk to him about the nature spirits: the earth-spirits (gnomes); the water-spirits (nymphs or naiads); the spirits of the air (sylphs), and the spirits of fire (salamanders), and tell him about the work these spirits do in the universe. But more important than anything else, they must instil in him a sense of the divine world, and a good way to begin is to talk about the Tree of Life and the Heavenly Hierarchies.

Of course, you have to put yourself on a child's level. There is no point in reeling off all the Cabbalistic names on the Sephirotic Tree of Life, but it is simple to give him the notion of hierarchy. You can begin by telling him, 'You see, men are more intelligent than animals, that is why they are above them,' and then you can explain why. 'And even amongst men and women, some are above others because they are better or wiser.' A child recognizes the truth of this. Then you can say, 'So why shouldn't there be other beings who are above men, even above the best and wisest?' A child accepts this, and in this way you introduce him to the notion of the existence of angels and archangels and all the entities of the spiritual Hierarchies. Any child who has been brought up like this will have a consciousness of a higher world of light and wisdom and the desire to strive towards it.

Anyone who denies the existence of worlds beyond our world and of living beings of a higher order than ours, confines himself and condemns himself to remain in darkness. And if so many people never advance or improve it is because they do not know, or refuse to admit, that beyond and above the human race, there is a whole hierarchy of sublime beings, angels and archangels, all the way to the Throne of God. And the result, of course, is that they have no goal or high ideal to cling to and from which to draw inspiration and energy of a higher order.

They go on living, of course, but from a spiritual point of view they never make any progress. They even refuse to accept the idea of a Master who could instruct and enlighten them. In fact many people are dead – spiritually dead. Whereas those who consciously accept the spiritual hierarchies have a higher goal in life and the impetus to do far greater things.

10

LOVE WITHOUT WEAKNESS

Thought for the Day:

'Fathers and mothers should never give way to their children's whims. They must be full of tenderness and love but inflexible. When they tell a child to do something they must be sure that he obeys. Some mothers give way to their child because he cries and they cannot bear to let him suffer. This is unintelligent pity because, later on, a child who has never learned to obey will have no respect for his parents. A mother must remain calm and gentle, never get angry and never hit her child, but she must not give way either, exactly like Mother Nature who never yields to the whims and wishes of human beings.

'If a child puts his fingers into a flame or onto a block of ice, the physical laws of heat and cold will not be changed to spare him. Nature looks on completely unmoved by what he does and this is why he learns to respect her. For a child, his mother represents nature and if she fails to do so faithfully he will never learn that certain limits must not be overstepped and he will be headed for catastrophe. A mother's weakness is very often the cause of children turning into complete scoundrels later on in life.

Yes, it is very often the unintelligent love of parents that causes so much distress in families, because they are incapable of teaching their children that there are certain laws which everyone must obey, parents and children alike. A child who is always allowed to do whatever he wants will never know the difference between good and evil, and it will not be his own fault: he was badly brought up. A child has to start learning that there are laws which he must obey when he is still very young, and it is up to his parents to teach him. 'But the poor little darling, what can I do if he cries?' Let him cry!

As soon as a child cries his mother gives way because she cannot bear to see her little darling unhappy; if she does this she is finished, she will be a slave and spend the rest of her life giving in to him. He will browbeat her and cause her great unhappiness, all because she did not know the difference between love and weakness. Your child cries? Let him cry, it will do his lungs good and he will begin to understand that there are rules which he has to respect and obey. If you relent at the first sign of tears, he will learn to use those tears to force you to give him his way. You must realize that a child is more intelligent and far more cunning than his mother! He very soon learns to use his tears to get his own way, and once he has got it he becomes unbearable. What can you expect? This is how mothers learn!

Parents should not wait before making it quite clear to their child that they have no intention of obeying his every whim and fancy, otherwise, by the time they decide to react it will be too late. Some parents, when they realize that the situation is serious, suddenly become strict and inflexible and a terrible battle ensues. They even beat their child! But it is too late: the damage is done and he has become completely intractable because they waited too long. They should have been firm with him from the beginning. Parents must learn to overcome the weakness that stems from their desire to give their child pleasure because he is little: in doing this they arouse very bad tendencies in his heart and soul. They should do just the opposite because it is when he is very young that he will accept restrictions, orders and rebukes. Later on when he is old enough to understand, he will love his parents for it and be grateful to them for sparing him a lot of suffering.

Some parents can never do enough to give their children pleasure and amuse them, and the result of this exaggerated desire to please can be catastrophic. Take the question of toys, for instance. What kind of toys are made nowadays for children to play with? Revolvers, tanks, guns and arms of all kinds, even miniature guillotines! And what do parents do? Instead of joining forces to protest and put a ban on such toys, they buy them! This is how they prepare their children to turn out badly. What unbelievable ignorance and stupidity! Has it never occured to them that these bloodthirsty games will necessarily have repercussions on the child's behaviour and mentality? Some children become monsters because they have been wrongly brought up by people with no knowledge of Initiatic Science.

Yesterday I saw a child making a hideous face and I asked his mother, 'Where did he learn to do that?' 'Oh,' she said; 'his father did it one day to amuse him so now he copies him.' Just look at how people educate their children! To amuse them and make them laugh they make a horrible grimace and, naturally, the children imitate them. You must never show anything ugly and stupid to your children just to amuse them! There are other ways of amusing them.

Parents should never do anything that is not educational and intelligent, even if it does not please their child. It is the child's place to accept and learn to adjust. Nowadays, nobody thinks of anything but pleasure. Pleasure is the very worst counsellor. It degrades man and causes him to sink back to the level of animals. Parents who are ignorant try to give pleasure to their children because of what they call their love. But there is more than one kind of love and you must choose the love which educates, refines and strengthens your child so that he will become perfect. Human beings are by nature selfish and ungrateful and it is this selfishness and ingratitude which over-indulgent parents encourage. Because you love your children you want to give them everything, but if you are wise you will deprive them of certain things.

I could go on talking all day but I know that parents would still not agree with me because my advice goes against their own methods. But isn't it obvious that they have problems with their children? And isn't it reasonable to think, therefore, that they would do well to revise those methods?

In the text which I read at the beginning I said that you should never hit your children. In point of fact, in exceptional cases, a slap or a good spanking does no harm. But there is one thing you have to be very careful about if you beat your child and that is your expression, the way you look at him. Your eyes must not express anger or hostility or negative feelings towards him, because although he will quickly forget the spanking, he will never forget it if you look at him with hostility. He will bear a grudge and sooner or later try to revenge himself. Be very careful of what your eyes express if you have to beat your child!

Often parents slap a child because he exasperates them and they lose patience, but this is a very bad reaction. Corporal punishment should never be the expression of a parent's exasperation – exasperation is not educational – but only to make the child understand that there are certain rules which have to be obeyed. This is the reason for a method which I know some of you find bizarre: when a mother has to punish her child she must be in full control of herself and show him that she hates having to hit him. She should even let him see her cry and tell him, 'I don't want to beat you but I have to because you have done wrong and you have to be punished for it.' Then she can go ahead with the spanking! In this way the child understands that his mother is unhappy, that it hurts her to have to beat him and that it is his own fault if she is obliged to punish him. This will make him reflect and understand that there are certain laws which must not be broken.

I insist on this point because I know that many parents do not pay much attention to the way in which they punish their children. Never, never strike them in anger because it leaves an impression of hatred and evil, not of justice, and it is essential for their proper education that children feel that their father and mother are just and that it is because they are just that they punish them. To strike a child in a fit of anger is very bad from the point of view of magic. Let me explain why.

When you strike a child in anger, the negative, disharmonious vibrations of your feelings are communicated to him, the anger which goes out from you in the form of a current of hostility will continue to work destructively on your child for months and even years and this is how, without realizing it, you give your child over to the control of negative forces. You see how ignorant parents are! Instead of helping and protecting their children they destroy something divine and sacred within them and fill them with the negative forces lurking in their own hearts. Parents must banish all angry reflexes from their conduct.

We cannot educate all the mothers and fathers of the earth but I hope that at least those who are members of the Brotherhood will accept the light of this Teaching. Let them punish their children when necessary, but without the destructive feelings which expose them to the influence of the powers of darkness. For there is another point I have not explained and that is that later on when they want to guide their children, they will find they cannot: they have no influence on them. Instead of being docile and obedient to their parents, the children obey only the spirits of darkness; it is they who have become their guides. You must give all this a lot of thought. Punish your children if you have to but only to make them aware that there are certain laws which they cannot disobey without endangering themselves.

This is how Nature behaves. Suppose it is winter and very cold and you break a window: unless you mend it you will have to put up with the consequences and spend your time shivering. If you appeal to Nature, 'I'm cold! couldn't you make it a little warmer?' she will remain completely unmoved and implacable. It is up to you to realize that you have been clumsy and repair the damage and not be so awkward in the future. A mother should treat her child in the same way as Nature treats us: by being unmoved and relentless and at the same time, showing him that she too obeys the same laws. In doing so she will inculcate in him the notion of order and hierarchy: you can expect wonders from a child who has been brought up in awareness and respect for the law.

Obviously, children are not all the same. In bringing them up you have to make allowances for their different degree of evolution, their temperament, their health and many other factors besides. There are so many different cases that one cannot establish a blanket rule for everyone. It is up to the parents to study their children and prove themselves sufficiently intelligent and enlightened to choose the method which best suits each one.

One thing is true and applicable in all cases and that is that parents must themselves be irreproachable and betray no faults or failings in front of their children. In the case of young mothers who have lovers or, during the war for instance, when women made love in the fields with soldiers of the army of occupation, they could not leave their small children alone in the house so they took them with them and, of course, they saw everything without understanding. But a few years later they remembered and understood, and the devastation caused by the scene they had witnessed became apparent in their attitude towards their mother. Why do mothers have to be so stupid and selfish? They do all kinds of negative things in the presence of their children, thinking that they do not see what is going on. Ah, but they do see, and everything is recorded in their subconscious. People can never forget some of the things they experienced when they were three, four or five years old. They forget what happened yesterday but they never forget something they experienced sixty or eighty years ago.

When parents show their failings, children are troubled and disoriented, they have nothing to hold onto anymore. Instinctively, children need to lean on someone who incarnates justice, nobleness, strength and perfection. They have an inborn sense of justice and truth, and when they see their parents behaving immorally, something inside them is deeply affected. A child knows that he is little and weak and he needs to feel the protection of an infallible authority over him. He may be ignorant, but he knows that he needs protection and this is why he presses up against his mother to feel her warmth. But the support he needs is not only physical, it is also psychological: when a child senses that his father and mother are not equal to their task, either he is lost or he rebels. Countless tragedies begin this way.

A child needs his parents to show strength, not weakness, and this is why, once you have given a child an order it is very bad to allow him to disobey. When parents give their child an order they must see to it that he obeys, otherwise he will realize that they are not firm and reliable and the image he has of them will compromise his education.

While we are on this subject I would like to talk to you about something very interesting. When an adult wants to do something, he starts by thinking about it, but a child's brain is not yet capable of reflection, for him action comes first, and this means that he should do what adults tell him without discussion. His mode of action is the exact opposite of an adult's. If a child had to understand before acting, he would never get anything done. He has to act before he understands. Others have understood before him and if he trusts their understanding, the development of his own process of understanding will be greatly facilitated.

Children can become intelligent by doing what their parents tell them, because true intelligence is action. Any achievement on the physical plane implies an intelligence behind its realization and when something is well done, one is led to the conclusion that it is the work of an intelligent being. Whether that intelligent being is visible or invisible, conscious or unconscious is quite another matter.

So, a child must do as he is told without explanations. When a mother takes her little boy
out with her she does not have to explain exactly
where they are going, he trusts her and lets her
take him by the hand knowing that she will not
lead him to where snakes, bears or wild boars
will tear him to pieces – symbolically speaking –
and this is how he develops and makes progress. But a child who cannot trust his parents or
who insists on being free and independent does
not develop his intelligence.

You will start raising all kinds of objections,
'Yes, but we know families in which the children
are far more intelligent than their parents. No
wonder they refuse to obey them.' I know that
every now and then there are exceptional children, but they are rare – very rare. I am speaking
generally and, in general, I simply do not believe
what so many people would like me to believe:
that most children are little geniuses who are
justified in rebelling against their mediocre parents. It is not true! A child is born into a particular family for a reason and since he is there, it
is too late to criticize and condemn. If he is such
a genius why did he choose to be born into such
a family? He has been born into this particular
family because he has something to learn from
them and to do this he must obey his parents.
Later on he will prove himself, like the princes

of royal blood who were sent into the army as simple soldiers so as to be treated (or rather ill-treated) like the others.

A child has no business, therefore, to argue and criticize. No one has asked him to create disorder and anarchy. Since he is there in that family he has to begin by living in harmony with his parents. When he has proved his superiority he can do as he likes, not before. When a child obeys his parents and does as they tell him, his intelligence begins to develop and gradually he will understand the reasons.

Of course, there are cases where the parents' unbending severity can be catastrophic. Take the case of a child who wants to do something on the spiritual level, but whose parents are so gross and ignorant, or dishonest enough to refuse him because it is incomprehensible to them. By their unyielding attitude they do him a great deal of harm. So, although there is a general rule, one must also take into account the exceptions and circumstances which may alter things.

Before making up their minds, before allowing or categorically refusing permission for something, parents should foresee and evaluate the circumstances of their decision. How can they do this if they have no discernment? They must begin by finding out what is involved before pronouncing judgment, for there are several factors to consider: whether the child is strong enough, whether it is the right moment, whether it will be for his good, whether he has a special gift which should be safeguarded, or not. In the area of food, for instance, parents should take a number of elements into account and not force their children to eat something just because they themselves think it's good.

I repeat, a mother and father should not demand absolute obedience from their child before asking themselves a certain number of questions, 'Is what we are asking of him good, just and divine? Is it what his soul needs or will it be detrimental to his evolution?' Once they have all the elements in hand and clearly understand what is good for the child, then they can make a categorical and irrevocable decision. And be it a permission or a refusal, he must accept their verdict.

A child should understand that there are laws which his parents also must obey. Even Initiates obey the great laws of nature – in fact they are the first to respect and obey them. They have a little less respect for man-made laws which may not always be just, but they are always full of respect and submission towards the eternal, universal laws of God. It is this spirit of respect and submission that the disciples of the Universal White Brotherhood must cultivate in themselves and hand on to their children.

I hope you understand me correctly: that you must love your children deeply goes without saying, but you must also know when and how to show your love. There are moments when it is better to show not love but wisdom. And only if you are capable of doing this can you talk about enlightened and beneficial love. Weak, foolish love is a disaster for all concerned!

11

EDUCATION VERSUS INSTRUCTION

I

I am often asked for advice about how to educate children and I reply, 'As you know, a great deal has been done in recent years concerning children and adolescents, but if you look at the improvements in the schools and so on, you will see that they all concern the external, material side. The schools are bigger and better and equipped with laboratories, radio, cinema, television, sports grounds, swimming-pools, etc. Yes, but what about the children? Are they any better? I'm afraid not!'

In the past, people attached less importance to the exterior aspects. Any old house, even a stable, would do as a school. The wind whistled through gaps in the windows stuffed with paper. No wood was provided: each child arrived with his own log for the fire. Sometimes there were no books for the pupils; the only person to have one was the teacher. And yet, out of these schools came exceptional men and women, strong, noble characters who could be taken as models. Nowadays the material conditions have been vastly improved but what are the schools turning out? A lot of lying, self-seeking, dishonest, rude rascals! Oh, they are very well-informed, that is true! They can dazzle you with information, but beneath the surface, in their characters, you cannot count on any solid, noble qualities.

Shall I tell you about the conditions I had when I went to school? My father died when I was very young and we were very poor, so poor that my mother could not afford to buy books. Very often I went off to school in the morning with no breakfast and I was always a bit drowsy in class – sometimes I fell asleep. During the recreation periods I borrowed my class-mates' books and, in a great hurry, tried to learn a little of the day's lesson and then, when the teacher called on me I had to try to remember what I had read in those few minutes. In retrospect I see that all those difficulties I had to contend with awoke certain qualities in my character which stood me in good stead later on. When life is too comfortable it chloroforms us and puts us to sleep. Those who have brought great benefits to mankind have never been people who were comfortably established. Rich people who have everything they need in life – just look in what they are interested, what they talk about: trivialities!

Some of you may object: 'Yes, but these schools which are so well equipped nowadays are very useful. Thanks to all that equipment our children can learn to be technicians and engineers, etc.' True! They can learn whatever you like on the technical level. But is mankind any happier because of technical progress, comfort or speed? I am certainly not opposed to progress but you have to be sure that you're 'progressing' in the right direction! At the moment, men and women are only interested in improving material conditions as though there were no other areas in which they needed to improve. I am all in favour of progress – but what kind? In spite of all the technical progress of the last few decades the quality of life has not improved. People are no happier than they were before; they are no less troubled and anxious; they are no more radiant with inner light than they were in the past; their health is no better.

The desire to improve exterior conditions is very praiseworthy, to be sure, but in doing so it is the inner aspects, the characters of the young, which have been forgotten. Teachers, professors and parents thought that all children needed was to have better books and learning-aids but these have not produced the miraculous results hoped for. Of course many people are aware of this. They realize that in spite of all the recent improvements and no matter how much the children are reprimanded and punished, they are not getting any better. On the contrary. Why? Because they have no living examples before them.

The only way to get good results in education is for teachers and educators to be models for the children. The first and most important educators are parents, and if they betray their vocation, if they fail to practise what they preach, the children will very soon realize that something is not right; when this happens not only do the parents lose all authority but their children begin to follow their example. They learn that truth is a coin which has two sides : one for public consumption and one for private use and that you can do whatever you like as long as you do not lose face. They all practise deceitfulness and fraud because this is the example they have before their eyes.

Nowadays, the majority of educators are intellectuals who have no real vocation for their profession : they have acquired a smattering of superficial knowledge from all the books they have read but on the inside they are not really pedagogues. A true pedagogue is born not made, and his mere presence, the light in his eyes, the emanations which flow from him are sufficient to educate children. History holds more than one example of men or women who were born with that special love, that special moral quality which has such a profound influence on children. For children are sensitive. They are like animals which can sense if a man is their master or not, even from a distance. Take the case of horses for instance: if a rider is cowardly his horse senses it and in no time at all the horseman is unhorsed! For anyone else the same horse may be perfectly docile. And children have the same intuition.

However, more and more teachers and professors are beginning to question their educational methods and before long they will understand that the only way to educate young people and have a good influence on them is to be blameless oneself. Why is this? Because as I was saying, children have a special sense, like animals, and generally their judgment is unerring. This is why, although I never fear the judgment of an adult I tremble before a child's judgment. It is terrifying! The opinion of children is very important to me because I know that they have an instinct for truth.

When I was a college student in Varna during the First World War, as most of the teachers had been called to the Front we had substitute

teachers to take the classes while they were
away. One year we had two different mathematics teachers one after the other. Whenever the
first one came into the schoolroom the whole
class erupted in pandemonium, the pupils began
to laugh and play the fool and, although he did
all he could to restore order, shouting and
threatening and gesticulating, it was all to no
avail. He would even go and fetch the Principal,
but as soon as his back was turned the uproar
began again. And yet that teacher was a very
nice man. I was sorry for him and I could not
understand why my classmates were so cruel. In
fact, one day I was so indignant at their attitude
that, while he was absent I spoke to the class and
told them that they were being inconsiderate.
They agreed to mend their ways and for a couple
of days it was better, but then the bedlam began
all over again. It was as though the teacher's attitude, or something in his emanations, triggered
the pupils' reaction and made them turbulent.

One day he left the school and was replaced
by a funny little man who came quietly into the
classroom without even looking at us. As soon
as he appeared, the pupils went to their places
without a word and never stirred during the
whole lesson. The teacher put his register on the
desk and in a very quiet voice, began the lesson.
He never got angry, never threatened us, never

punished anyone. He knew his subject inside-out, he never hesitated, and we were obliged to work very hard. I was fifteen or sixteen at the time and this made a great impression on me. I never forgot this little man who looked so completely insignificant, not because he was so knowledgeable but because of something in his presence, something which emanated from him and impressed us all. And this happens in schools and universities: every now and then you meet a professor who, without doing anything special to impress his students, commands respect simply by his presence.

There are other cases, for instance, of certain yogis in India who live in the jungle in the midst of tigers and cobras, and the animals never harm them: because of their innate purity and virtues the yogis give off powerful vibrations which the animals can sense and which keep them at a respectful distance, whereas they would attack anyone else.

If instruction is so highly rated nowadays it is because everyone knows that it is the key to the best, most prestigious and most highly paid positions. In the meantime, the child's education is neglected because it brings none of these advantages. In fact someone who gives priority to moral values will almost always be ousted by unscrupulous individuals who have learned to look out for themselves; besides, it is much more demanding to work at improving one's character than to acquire a university degree!

In any case parents are at fault here, too. Of course they are delighted to have obedient, sincere, respectful and honest children, but they are even more delighted if their children come top of their class or if they can attract attention by reciting a poem or playing something on the piano. What really matters for parents is the intellectual capacity of their children, not their moral qualities. I have seen this with my own eyes and I know that it is so. And later, when the children become knowledgeable, erudite adults, they turn against their parents, and criticize and blame them. The unfortunate parents are completely bewildered, they sacrificed so much to give their children a first-class schooling only to be met with nothing but criticism.

This is why I always tell parents, 'If you don't want all that instruction you are giving your children to be used against you one day, you must accept the Teaching of Initiatic Science. If you do, you yourself will become better in every way, more luminous and more radiant, and in that way you will impress your children a hundred times more than all their educators.'

Parents must not think that they are satisfying the essential needs of their children when they provide them with instruction. This is an illusion which can only lead to war between the generations: at school the children learn all kinds of things their parents never learned, and when they get home, armed with their diplomas and their so-called superiority, they give their parents a very hard time! And the parents are unhappy and disappointed to see that their children are ungrateful, rude and violent. But they have only themselves to blame! Why have they never done anything to acquire the inner light and strength that will always impress the children with their superiority? This should be the goal of all parents: to become so noble and high-minded, so radiant and strong that they will be exemplary.

If parents really want to hold on to their children, if they really want their children to love and admire them and never forsake them, then they must be an inspiration and example to them. If parents fail to do this, I warn them, they will lose their children. If they always look for the easy way out they will only get weaker and more vulnerable, and when a serious problem arises they will break down completely. What good will that be to anyone? Never let yourself reach that stage. Think about these things and do what you must do to overcome each difficulty as it arises.

Modern society is full of anomalies which are the result of the exaggerated importance attributed to instruction. Obviously, it is necessary, indispensable, but it has reached a point where children and adolescents are being stuffed with a surfeit of useless knowledge. As soon as they have finished their studies and passed their exams the first thing they do is to forget it all! What is the point of working so hard and for so long to accumulate a mass of information which will be forgotten almost at once, without ever learning what is essential in life? And what exactly is essential in life? I shall tell you, I will explain how Initiates look at this question of education.

Initiates see the human being as a kingdom in which the cells of the body are the population and the individual is the king. Unfortunately, in most instances, the king has been dethroned: his subjects have deposed him because he did not rule them wisely, he never instructed his cells how to carry out their appointed tasks, and instead of taking up the reins of government, he spent all his time in the pursuit of pleasure and had none left to devote to his people. Whilst he was engaged in useless, even criminal activities, his friends and associates saw nothing wrong and even admired him. But he could not conceal the truth from his subjects, his cells, who watched and waited until, at last, they decided to over-throw their unworthy sovereign.

The cells of our bodies are alive and en-dowed with intelligence; they watch us. As they are permanently in contact with us we cannot escape their vigilance, the least little deceit or dishonesty leaves its imprint on them and, be-fore long, they begin to follow the example we give them. They say to each other, 'Come on, it's quite all right to drink and plunder, the boss does it!' Nobody realizes that our cells follow the example we give them.

Before launching into the education of others, each individual must become the educa-tor of his own cells, in the belief that a popula-tion whose king gives a bad example will imitate him and end by dethroning him. A king who gives an example of kindheartedness, nobleness and integrity, will be imitated by his cells, they will sustain him and become so obedient and ra-diant that their light will manifest itself external-ly. It is this inner radiance, these emanations which influence human beings, animals and even plant-life

Whatever a man creates within himself by his work, his meditation and his purity, is re-flected first of all on his own cells; in a second

phase it manifests itself outwardly and influences other people. If you do not know this
law you will never accomplish anything authentic, for everything must first of all be created and
organized inside before taking shape on the
physical level.

Never forget that your example, good or bad,
before it influences others influences your own
cells ; when they see that your life is anarchistic
they too become anarchistic and refuse to obey
you. Try as you might, when you want to im-
pose your will on them they will refuse to listen
and you will find that you have no control over
your sensuality, your anger, your greed, etc.
Whereas if you succeed in gaining the respect
and trust of your cells you will have great power
over them. If you feel upset for instance, after a
few minutes of concentration you will be able to
recover your inner peace and light.

So, if you have shown a bad example to your
cells up to now, from now on change your inner
attitude and your behaviour. Your cells will register the improvement and will imitate you.
Obviously, to begin with, your new behaviour
will feel unnatural, but little by little it will become more natural, you will find yourself constantly helped and stimulated to do even better.

When a man has accomplished this educational work with his own children, the cells

within his own body, then he can undertake to educate others exterior to himself, whether children or adult men and women. Then his words and example will ring true : instead of being hollow and empty he will be full of power, vibrant and alive. People will sense that he is a true pedagogue : his integrity and unity, his authenticity will make themselves felt. Yes, and this is because his 'subjects' within uphold his authority and give him strength so that there is magic in his presence. Whatever he says gets results because his whole being is unified, accustomed to working in one direction. He is not divided in himself, pulling one way outwardly and another way inwardly.

We all have to attain this kind of integrity, this unity : what we manifest must be the authentic expression of what we are inside. When we reach this stage we can be extremely effective educators. True power is when every single cell emanates something authentic ; otherwise only that part of us which speaks expresses a little light, everything else in us cries out, 'No, no ! It's not true !'

Real magic exists only where there is truth and unity. Magic presupposes unification, a mustering of forces and energies ; there can be no magic in the presence of dispersion and dislocation. But although I am saying this about magic you must understand that it is not really magic that interests me. I never read books on magic or sorcery although I did glance through some at one time just to have an idea of what they said, but I have no time to waste on this kind of reading. No! For me, magic is life; magic is the whole universe. This is the true treatise on magic, and it is lying open before us, waiting for us to read it – but we still haven't learned to read!

In practice there are three categories of educators: those who demand that their students respect and obey certain rules, although it is obvious that they themselves have no respect for anything; those who are careful to give a good example in public but who do so out of pride or vanity to protect their reputation and don't mind breaking the rules in private; and finally, the third category, Initiates, the true educators, who are not inwardly divided: what they teach, what they aspire to is an expression of themselves, it is part of them, their very quintessence. This is the goal we must reach.

And this is why, for me, the greatest of all pedagogues is the sun. Yes, it is the sun who is my Master. Do you know what he told me one day? He said, 'Believe me, all those so-called pedagogues know nothing of true pedagogy. They don't even know that if you want to warm someone you have to be warm yourself and if you want to communicate light and life to someone you have to be luminous and alive yourself. Educators try to force the young to develop moral qualities which they themselves don't possess and which they are incapable of demonstrating in their own behaviour. How can you expect the young not to rebel? It's normal that they should refuse to obey people like that!' There – that's what the sun says!

A true pedagogue manifests in his behaviour the qualities he wants to instil in others; something contagious, stimulating and irresistible must flow from him. A true poet or musician stimulates others to be poets or musicians; someone whose heart overflows with love inspires others to love; a daring, courageous officer influences the men under his command, he launches an attack and they follow him to victory over the enemy. Can an officer call on his men to follow him into battle if his voice is shaking with fear? No one would obey him! Educators tell the young, 'Be kind; be honest; be this that or the other', but what about them? Do they practise what they preach? How can you expect young people to obey?

Education today is concerned only with the surface, with trivia, whereas true education is concerned with the inner centre, the core of things. If you are inwardly noble, just and honest, then without having to say one word you will inspire those around you to be noble, just and honest too.

The magical power of pedagogy lies in one thing and one thing only: example. I cannot repeat this too often. All the rest is trimmings, stuff and nonsense! Teachers 'know' a great deal; they read, write, explain and expound all kinds of clever theories, but they are incapable of being living examples. That's not good enough! I never read books on education any longer, there are too many of them and they all contradict each other anyway. If you asked me about educational programmes in other countries or the latest educational systems and trends, I would have to admit that I know nothing about all that. All my energy, all my willpower is concentrated on one central goal: how to become a model, a living example. Only that!

II

If teachers and professors are worn out at the end of the school year it is not because it is so exhausting to take care of children but because all too often they work with a mercenary mentality: their main concern is to earn their living. They are not interested in the children. They simply try to get through their work as quickly as possible, never stopping to reflect on the exalted nature of their calling which is to look after the souls of all these children that Heaven has entrusted to their care. It goes without saying that children have failings, but once you embark upon the career of an educator you assume the obligation to think of the children's future, to be attentive and considerate towards them, in fact to love them. And as all children are responsive to affection and gentleness, after a time they will begin to respond and to change.

When I was still in Bulgaria, more than fifty years ago, I knew a very old woman who had

never learned to read and write. Towards the
end of her life, when she was seventy years old,
she asked to go to the village school. She lived in
a small village and the schoolmaster agreed to let
her join the class. Well, you can just imagine the
children's reaction when they saw an old lady
sitting in the classroom with them! They did
nothing but tease and laugh at her. And she?
Not only did she never get angry with them, but
she would hug and kiss them and bring them little presents. Before long the children stopped
laughing at her. They adored her. And one day,
when she had got a chill and could not go to
school, the whole class trooped off to her house
to beg her to get better quickly and come back to
school with them. They did not want to learn
their lessons if she was not there.

Yes, but if you want to have this kind of effect on children you need a great deal of love and
patience. The world has had a few great educators such as Pestalozzi for instance, who was not
especially learned but who achieved amazing results with difficult children because of his great
love. But such people are rare. I know what a
tremendous job it is to educate children, if I can
talk to you about this it is because I, too, have
been first a teacher and later the principal of a
college in Bulgaria, and I have seen with my own
eyes the effect of love and patience on children.

Because of all the tales my pupils used to tell their parents about me, they would often come and see me to thank me and bring me presents. In fact I had so many presents that in the end I did not know what to do with them or where to put them all! When I left to come to France, they all came to the station and cried to see me go! I can never forget that. I often think of all those children who are grandfathers and grand-mothers by now!

If educators and teachers made a conscious effort to introduce spiritual elements into the hearts and souls of their pupils they would never be forgotten, for those elements remain alive and active in the children's souls and they will al-ways remember the men and women who gave them something so precious. As things are now children don't even remember who their teachers were, or if they remember it is usually only to laugh at them or even detest them still, years later. So all their work is wasted and use-less because there was no love or light in it, no awareness of its true grandeur.

A teacher who really loves the children does not get so exhausted because his nervous system is not under such strain. But you must work with love and patience, you must be convinced that your work will be a success and that it will win you friends who will never forget you, otherwise you will be fighting a losing battle. Love is particularly important when you are dealing with little children because the friends you will be making are their Guardian Angels. Every child has a Guardian Angel who takes care of him, watches over him and does his best to educate him. But his task is often made extremely difficult because of all the other influences the child is subject to. The Angels watch over their charges but they can't do everything for them so they are delighted when they see that someone else is trying to help and they will see that he gets his reward. By your good work, therefore, you win the friendship not only of the children and their parents – for children always tell their parents all about their teachers – but also of the children's Guardian Angels. Instead of trying to get rid of your pupils as quickly as you can, isn't it worth making an effort and taking some trouble with them? If you do not think so you would do much better not to be an educator: choose another profession!

As you can see there are certain methods you must know about in order to work with children. You could say that you should not even think of them, but only of yourself; if you do not want to end up exhausted and in a state of collapse, keep calm, be more patient and attentive and you will save a lot of energy. If you are always tense and irritable you will end by falling ill.

A lot of teachers spend their time heaping abuse on the children because they cannot get them to improve. Are they themselves such shining examples, are they justified in wanting to change others? Most of them are so common-place and mediocre, how can they have the nerve to undertake the education of children? It is not their vocation. They were cut out to be butchers, and now look at them: educators! It has never occurred to them that their task is to work on the souls and spirits of their pupils and leave the imprint of something divine in them. Tell me, where is the university that reveals to future educators the power of love? Where can students learn that love is the only way to transform, educate and improve human beings?

As I have always maintained, the best and most noble of all professions is that of pedagogue or educator. Of course, not everybody shares my opinion. In fact people have no great respect for this profession nowadays. If you are a physicist, a lawyer or a doctor – now that's different! There is prestige attached to those professions! But schoolmasters and teachers? People are in-clined to look down on them. They don't think that looking after children amounts to much! Well, that is where they are very mistaken, because this is the most meaningful and most important of all professions. The education of children is divine work!

I hear that people, these days, are focussing more and more attention on the subject of human nature and the psychology and education of human beings. This is because they have begun to realize that there can be neither success nor lasting happiness for mankind as long as these questions are not properly understood. Before long people will be talking of nothing else. The only trouble is that there is a big difference between the realization that something has to be changed in this area and the ability to bring about the necessary changes. Look at politics! Everybody talks about change: this must be changed and that should be changed... It is easy to talk but when one has not prepared oneself to bring about the necessary changes it is simply grotesque to talk like that!

So, it is not enough to spend three or four years at a university to be ready to assume the responsibility of an educator. A whole lifetime of study, in fact several lifetimes are necessary for the key to education lies in Initiatic Science. An educator must have something special in his heart and soul and spirit: the sacred flame of the born teacher which throbs and glows and reaches out to influence others. In the presence of a true pedagogue other people are seized with a desire to imitate him even before he has opened his mouth. They sense that there is something luminous and warm, something alive in him and it is that warmth and light and that life which helps them to understand whatever he explains to them.

We never influence people much by a great display of knowledge. Knowledge is, of course, a very useful and potent instrument: a great many things can be understood if we have good, clear arguments at our command. But this is not enough, for even when people understand they are not necessarily moved. The only forces which stimulate and inspire others are love, faith and conviction. These are living forces. Love and faith combined, these are true power! When you are faced with difficulties in life, if you have plenty of intellectual learning and nothing else, you will remain irresolute, weak and apprehensive, but if you have love and faith, even if you are not very well-informed, you will never be defeated. You will continue to advance, to rise to greater heights and to overcome all the obstacles you meet on your way.

In the Gospels it says, 'If you had faith even the size of a mustard seed, you could say to that mountain, "Remove yourself", and it would be gone.' This is symbolic, of course. Jesus did not mean that human beings should start moving mountains, they are all right where they are : no need to try to put them somewhere else! Leave the mountains alone, for Nature in her wisdom has placed them exactly where they should be to transmit certain currents and forces. The mountains which Jesus was talking about are the mountains of obscurity, selfishness and sloth in our minds and hearts and wills. We forget about these and want to start attacking the beautiful, innocent mountains created by the Lord! Did Jesus remove mountains? He never wasted his time on things like that, and yet he did move mountains. In fact he moved kingdoms and whole continents in the hearts and heads of human beings : he turned the whole world upside down.

Try to understand what I am telling you to-day : it is not enough to accumulate knowledge. You must go to work to acquire love, faith and audacity, otherwise you will always be weak. You will be like a bookworm who spends his whole life in libraries, so absorbed in books that he forgets to eat. He reads and reads and gets pale, sickly and lifeless, and before long, he is obliged to abandon everything, even his beloved books. Of course, if you prefer book-learning, go ahead. But you will become dry and withered and neither love nor kindness will emanate from you. You will be nothing but a cold, dried-up intellect which discusses, criticizes and dissects everything, but which is incapable of escaping from its own inner disorder.

This is one of the greatest dangers for philosophy students. By the time they finish their studies, they are disoriented by the jumble of contradictory systems and ideas they have had to study. Of course it is only to be expected, for in philosophical studies you will find everything except true philosophy. You learn about the brainstorms and flights of fancy concocted by human beings over centuries in all countries of the world, but very often these so-called philosophers were no more than average people, capable of seeing things only from their own very limited point of view. With the exception of those who possessed the true knowledge of the higher worlds (I mentioned them in my lecture about Ancient Egyptian Initiation), the thinkers whose works young people are obliged to study these days, end by unsettling them completely and by destroying their faith and their capacity to distinguish truth from falsehood.

What can one do with young people who believe in nothing any more and who live in disorder and chaos? Is that the purpose of philosophy? What good does it do them to know that one imbecile taught one thing and another taught just the opposite? Young people need to learn the one true philosophy, that which is found in the living Book of Nature. But their professors themselves have never studied that book, so all they can do is present a hodgepodge of ideas, some true and some false – and inevitably there is a great deal of falsehood and very little truth! Let me warn you that by continuing to use these methods the schools are preparing an uprush of anarchy and suicides amongst students.

Understand, therefore, that the only true philosophy is that which can give you life, love and faith and one must never, never abandon it for the sake of the latest speculations which, admittedly, may have the seduction of novelty but which have nothing worthwhile to offer you. The truth of this is so obvious: have these new philosophies made you stronger and more radiant? No! And that is because, instead of sinking your teeth into Life, instead of drinking great draughts of Light and delving deep into Truth, you have been content to make do with a few superficial details.

Everyone is at liberty to do what he pleases, but I know in advance what the results will be according to whether you nourish your minds with life or spend all your time immersed in books. So far you have not really grasped the difference between nourishing your minds and reading. For my part, I never read books, I have no time. But I read the Book of Nature and I read, too, what is written on your faces and in your hearts. And, above all, I read the sun, the sun is my daily reading. Every day he reveals something new to me and then I pass his revelations on to you. In time, you too will begin to read fewer books because you will have learned to read the Book of Living Nature.

In the morning, you begin with breakfast so as to have the strength to do all you have to do during the day. If you go to the library without breakfasting you will probably be too drowsy to understand what you are reading. You need strength in order to work; and to gain strength you must eat. Since this is so, why can't you understand that the same law applies on the spiritual level?

Learn to seek spiritual nourishment which is alive and fresh, and absorb it as you absorb the sun's rays at dawn. You need pure food direct from the source, a pure, simple, potent nourishment to fill you with light, quench your thirst and restore you to life; and this is what you get here. As I often say, this is not a university, it's a restaurant!

So, be glad, because even if you learn nothing new here, at least you receive the impetus of enthusiasm and life – and that is what matters. Before all else you must be alive. Later you can go and learn whatever you like!

can best succeed in their task of educating the child. He is far more deeply impressed by the way the people around him behave and are, than by any lesson or advice that he receives from time to time. Educating the child's subconscious requires a very high level of consciousness on the part of the educators.

204 – THE YOGA OF NUTRITION

This book is not a dietary handbook, it has nothing to do with diet. The Master Omraam Mikhaël Aïvanhov considers the way man thinks about the food more important than what, or how much, he eats. The Master lifts the act of eating onto the level of a mystical rite, a sacrament such as Holy Communion, the Last Supper, in all their spiritual significance.

Even someone to whom the spiritual aspect is foreign cannot but understand as he reads that his thoughts and feelings, his way of considering his daily nourishment, are what lead him to the profound mysteries of the relationship between man and Nature, the nature which nourishes him. If he deepens that relationship by extracting from the food the more subtle, finer elements, his entire being will then be able to unfold and flourish.

205 – SEXUAL FORCE OR THE WINGED DRAGON

The dragon, fabulous beast of Mythology and all Christian iconography, is not merely a relic of antiquity but a symbol of the human being's instinctive, primitive forces. The spiritual life is the process of learning how to subdue, control and direct these forces so that man will be propelled to the highest peaks of spirituality. The fire-breathing monster with the tail of a serpent has wings as well, indicating that the forces he embodies have a spiritual destination. The Master Omraam Mikhaël Aïvanhov says, "Sexual energy can be compared to petrol: if you are ignorant and careless you are burned by it, your very quintessence will be destroyed by this consuming force. The Initiates are those whose knowledge permits them to use the force to soar above the universe." That is the true meaning of the winged Dragon.

206 – THE UNIVERSAL WHITE BROTHERHOOD IS NOT A SECT

The very strong feelings of antipathy held by many of the general public on the subject of sects tend to hide the real problems of society. Indignation is felt against minorities who have decided to undertake a spiritual life apart from orthodox religious practice but non-conformity in other fields is looked upon with favour. The intellectual, political, social and economic fields are largely composed of many separate parts and groups which are, in effect, 'sects,' concerned with the triumph of their own particular theories or interests over those of their opponents. From now on a sect will no longer be defined in relation to the official church but in terms of the universality of its ideas in all fields. And if the Universal White Brotherhood is not a sect, it is precisely because its Teaching, which is directed to men of every race and religion and which encompasses every kind of human activity, aims at developing a consciousness of universality amongst all men.

207 – WHAT IS A SPIRITUAL MASTER?

Although the idea of a spiritual Master is becoming more and more familiar to the public, the nature and role of a Master are still poorly understood, even by those who claim to be disciples. The purpose of this book is essentially to shed light on the subject. This clarification may seem ruthless to some, but it is necessary, for what matters above all is not to delude oneself as to the realities of the spiritual life. It is true that a Master is that prodigious being capable of leading men towards the highest summits of the spirit, but for the Master as for his disciples, this exciting adventure can be successful only if it is accompanied by tremendous demands upon oneself.

208 – UNDER THE DOVE, THE REIGN OF PEACE

All the official steps taken in favour of peace seem to infer that it is a state which can be imposed on men from the outside... the creating of organizations for peace, reinforcing security means, the imprisonment or pure and simple suppression of troublemakers, for example. But what hope is there for peace when man continues to nourish within himself the seeds of all political, social and economic conflicts? These seeds are his uncontrolled desires for possession and domination. A better understanding of what peace truly is and the conditions necessary for achieving it are called for. As long as man doesn't make the decision to intervene on the battlefield of his disorderly thoughts and feelings, **he won't** be able to create a lasting peace.

209 – CHRISTMAS AND EASTER IN THE INITIATIC TRADITION

The Feasts of Christmas and Easter, celebrated annually throughout Christendom to commemorate the birth and resurrection of Jesus, actually are part of the initiatic tradition in existence long before the Christian era. Their appearance at those particular times of the year – the Winter solstice and the Spring equinox – is indicative of their Cosmic significance and also of the fact that man participates in the processes of gestation, birth and blossoming which take place in nature.

Christmas and Easter, the second birth and the resurrection, are really two different ways of celebrating the regeneration of man and his birth into the spiritual world.

210 – THE TREE OF THE KNOWLEDGE OF GOOD AND EVIL

The existence of evil in a world created by God who is perfect is an enigma which remains unsolved to this day by the world's philosophies or religions. Within the framework of Judeo-Christianism, Master Omraam Mikhaël Aïvanhov asserts that the solution lies in knowing what methods to use to contain evil, rather than in explanations or interpretations. Whatever its origin, evil is a reality which man confronts daily, both inwardly and outwardly. He must learn to deal with it. For him to fight against it is useless, even dangerous, for the odds are against him. He must be armed with *methods* of dealing with it, to overcome and transform it. This book offers those methods.

211 – FREEDOM, THE SPIRIT TRIUMPHANT

Freedom has become such a political stake that we have lost sight of the true terms through which man can find freedom. It is those terms, which are those of the relationship between spirit and matter, that the Master Omraam Mikhaël Aïvanhov attempts to restore. "No creature," he says, "can subsist without a certain number of elements that he receives from outside himself. God alone is not subject to this law; He has no need of anything external to Himself. But He has left a spark of Himself, a spirit identical to Him in nature, in every human being, and therefore man, thanks to his spirit, can create everything he needs. The Teaching I bring is that of the spirit, the Creator, and not that of matter and of creation. This is why I tell you that by entering the realm of the spirit which creates, forms and shapes matter, we will escape the hold the outside world has on us and be free."

212 – LIGHT IS A LIVING SPIRIT

Light offers infinite possibilities to us in the material and spiritual fields. It is seen by tradition as the living substance with which God created the world and in the last few years we have seen the development of the laser with all its potential. Omraam Mikhaël Aïvanhov invites us in this book to discover light's spiritual possibilities, to see how it can protect, nourish and teach us to know ourselves, nature and God, but above all he shows light as the only truly effective method of transforming ourselves and the world.

213 – MAN'S TWO NATURES, HUMAN AND DIVINE

To justify their failings and weaknesses, you hear people exclaim, "I'm only human!" What they should actually be saying is, "I'm only animal!" How, then, should we define human nature?

Man, that ambiguous creature placed by evolution on the border between the animal world and the divine world, has a double nature. To be able to advance further in his evolution he must become aware of this ambivalence. It says in the Holy Writ, "Ye are gods," which ought to remind man of the presence within of the higher essence which he must learn to manifest. "That is the real meaning of destiny," says Master Omraam Mikhaël Aïvanhov, "the true purpose and goal of our existence." This is why he comes back again and again to this question, giving us methods for us to learn and use in order to manifest ourselves as the gods we really are... but do not know yet.

214 – HOPE FOR THE WORLD:
SPIRITUAL GALVANOPLASTY

"Everything in the universe, in Nature and in man reflects the two fundamental principles, masculine and feminine. All Creation is the result of the two principles working together as a reflection of the creative cosmic principles, our Heavenly Father and our Divine Mother, Nature. Everywhere the two principles are at work, in Nature and in man, whose mind and spirit represent the male principle and whose heart and soul represent the feminine principle. One cannot work without the other, they are not productive when separated... which explains why men and women are constantly seeking each other.

"Spiritual Galvanoplasty is the science of the two principles applied to man's inner life."

Omraam Mikhaël Aïvanhov

215 – THE TRUE MEANING OF CHRIST'S TEACHING

In his lectures over the years, some of which form the contents of this book, the Maître Omraam Mikhaël Aïvanhov shows that Jesus condensed his entire Teaching into the prayer beginning with the words, "Our Father which art in heaven..." now called the Lord's Prayer. Initiates, says the Master, proceed as Nature does. A tree with its roots and trunk, branches, leaves, blossoms and fruit at first is no more than a minute seed but, if you plant it, water it and expose it to the sun, it becomes a majestic tree in all its splendour... because Nature in her wonderful way has condensed the tree's entire potential into the tiny seed. Jesus did the same. He took his Teaching, the new Science he was bringing mankind, and condensed it into a prayer to his Father in the hope that this seed would take root in men's souls, be nurtured by them with care, and grow into its potential : the massive, fruitful tree of the Initiatic Science, the real Teaching of Christ.

Omraam Mikhaël Aïvanhov

216 – THE LIVING BOOK OF NATURE

"We live in a civilisation which requires us to know how to read and write, and this is very good. It will always be necessary to read and write but we must also know how to do so on other planes. In Initiatic Science, to read means to be able to decipher the subtle and hidden side of objects and creatures, to interpret the symbols and signs placed everywhere by Cosmic Intelligence in the great book of the universe. To write means to leave one's imprint on this great book, to act upon stones, plants, animals and men through the magic force of one's spirit. It is not just on paper that we must know how to read and write but upon all regions of the universe."

Omraam Mikhaël Aïvanhov

217 – NEW LIGHT ON THE GOSPELS

The Gospel stories have always appealed to the reader because of the narrative form in which they are written. Even if they leave us in the dark concerning much of the life of Jesus, they give us absorbing details of his daily life and his Teaching in the form of allegories.

The Master Omraam Mikhaël Aïvanhov commands our interest by the way he interprets these brief allegorical tales, real or symbolic, treating them as psychological data and situations. The ten virgins going forth to meet the Bridegroom ; the rich landowner demanding an accounting from his steward ; the householder trying to find labourers for his fields ; the disciples in the ship awakening the sleeping Jesus in their terror at the storm ; the answer to the question of the tribute owed to 'Caesar' – these stories are stripped of their merely historical or picturesque aspects (which would limit their significance and importance to the purely external) and appear as actual problems of the inner life, real questions that arise in every man's innermost heart where the two great antagonists, the spiritual and the material forces, confront each other and must be reconciled.

218 – THE SYMBOLIC LANGUAGE OF
GEOMETRICAL FIGURES

'From the earliest days of history, men have sought a language which would be both universal and synthetic, a language capable of expressing the richest and most complex realities while, at the same time, reducing them to the barest essentials. It is this research that led to the discovery of figures and symbols.

Images and symbols can speak, they do have a language, which is essentially that of symbols of geometric figures. Symbolic figures are like a structure, the framework of reality. But these forms, even if reduced to a skeletal state, are nevertheless far from dead because they represent living realities in man and in the universe. That is why we have to put life into them and instil them with spirit if we want to interpret them; so long as we remain content to study them externally they will mean absolutely nothing to us.'

Omraam Mikhaël Aïvanhov

220 – THE ZODIAC, KEY TO MAN
AND TO THE UNIVERSE

This volume by the Master Omraam Mikhaël Aïvanhov is not an astrological handbook. The Zodiac here discussed is the Book of Books in which everything is recorded, and the constellations and planets are the hieroglyphs, the sacred letters which reveal, to those who know how to decipher them, how mankind and the world were created, how they evolve hand in hand and how their inner structure is identical. Every human being who becomes aware of his kinship with the universe begins to feel the need to cultivate his inner life in order to rediscover, within himself, that cosmic plenitude symbolized to perfection by the circle of the Zodiac.

EDITOR – DISTRIBUTOR

FRANCE   Editions PROSVETA S.A. – B.P. 12
       83601 Fréjus Cedex

DISTRIBUTORS

BRITISH ISLES PROSVETA Ltd. – The Doves Nest,

       Prosveta
      The Doves Nest J
       Duddleswell
       Uckfield
     East Sussex TN22 3JJ

       Dorset SP7 8PL

CANADA   PROSVETA Inc. – 1565 Montée Masson
       Duvernay est, Laval, Qué. H7E 4P2

DENMARK SANKT ANSGARS FORLAG
       Bredgade 67 – 1260 Copenhague

HOLLAND UITGEVERIJ SERVIRE B.V.
       Varkevisserstraat 52
       NL – 2225 Katwij aan Zee

HONG KONG HELIOS
       31 New Kap Bin Long Village
       Sai Kung N.T., Hong Kong

IRELAND   PROSVETA IRL.
       84 Irishtown – Clonmel

NORWAY   PROSVETA NORGE
       Husebyveien 8b
       0379 Oslo 3

UNITED STATES PROSVETA U.S.A. – P.O. Box 49614
       Los Angeles, California 90049